# Lighten Up!

(sung to the tune of "If You're Happy and You Know It")

*When life's got you overrun,*
*then lighten up.*
*Think of all the good you've done*
*and lighten up.*
*If your job is just half done and*
*Your big battle's just half won,*
*Pat yourself on half your back*
*and lighten up.*

*If you're feeling loaded down*
*then lighten up.*
*Shrug your shoulders, sing a song,*
*and lighten up.*
*With a friend or two beside you*
*And the Savior's love to guide you,*
*Let some sunshine back inside you—*
*Lighten up!*

# Lighten Up!

## CHIEKO N. OKAZAKI

Deseret Book
Salt Lake City, Utah

**Library of Congress Cataloging-in-Publication Data**

Okazaki, Chieko N., 1926–
    Lighten up! / Chieko N. Okazaki
      p.  cm.
    Includes index.
    ISBN 0–87579–668–0 (hard)
    1. Women–Religious life.  2. Women–Conduct of life.  I. Title.
BX8641.046  1993
248.8'.43–dc20= 92–40396

                                                  CIP

Printed in the United States of America

10   9   8   7   6   5

*To Ed,*
*my partner*

# Contents

# Rejoicing in Diversity

CHAPTER ONE

# Lighten Up!

I LOVE MY SISTERS in the Relief Society. My story may be unique in some aspects, but I am always amazed by how deeply we resemble each other and how much we have in common as women.

I grew up a child of humble Japanese laborers on a plantation on the big island of Hawaii. I put myself through high school by working as a maid for my room and board, and also worked my way through college. My parents were Buddhists. I joined the Church at the age of fifteen without their permission, though they later consented. I married a nonmember, who later joined the Church. Ed and I were able to have two children, then no more. We lived in Utah soon after World War II, where we had a hard time finding a home to buy or a lot to build on because we were Japanese. I worked most of my married life, first as an elementary schoolteacher, then as a principal, so I know about the challenges of balancing work and family responsibilities. I'm a triple cancer survivor. And I am still dealing with the bewildering reality of loneliness. My beloved partner, Ed, went on ahead on March 20, 1992, leaving me to follow alone. This hard experience was followed by two others just a few weeks later: I lost a grandchild only a few days before it was due to be born, and my brother was diagnosed as having a brain tumor.

I know I share many of these experiences with other women. I know there are many women throughout the Church who grew up in poverty. Women who have had to struggle and sacrifice to get an education. Women who have nonmember husbands or part-member families. Women who have dealt with infertility. Women who have felt the sting of racial prejudice. Women who have left the traditional religion of their families to embrace the gospel. Women who have worked outside their homes, either as a career choice or out of necessity. Women who bear the emotional and physical burdens of ill health. Women who are struggling with the loss of a loved one. I never had a biological sister, yet the more closely I work with women in the Church, the more surely I know there is a spiritual sisterhood.

We are all different and deal with diverse circumstances. Diversity is a strength, not a division. I attend a lot of meetings where I'm the only woman. And I attend many, many meetings where I'm the only Oriental woman. You can perhaps imagine how that feels. Have you ever had the feeling that you're the odd one, the different one? Maybe even too odd or different for this church? The truth is that you're not odd—you're special. When white light falls on a wall, it makes a white wall. But when it passes through a prism, that same light makes a rainbow on the wall.

What is a rainbow? It's light, though a special kind of light. What was the first thing God did in creating this beautiful earth for us? He said, "Let there be light." (Genesis 1:3.) The scriptures record, "And there *was* light." I'd like to say the same thing: "Let there be light." All kinds of light! Red, orange, yellow, green, blue, and violet light.

We need our differences. Diversity is important to us as individuals and as a church. Yet often we feel that our diversity is a problem—that we are wrong to be different, that we have nothing in common with a sister who has a different story, and that the gospel exists to make us all the same. We feel that if we have challenges or difficulties, we must be doing something wrong, and so we burden ourselves with extra guilt on top of the challenge.

I'd like to share with you my favorite Japanese proverb, which gives advice you might find helpful when life gets difficult. It's a short saying, and it comes from the ancient book of Okazaki, chapter one, verse one:

Lighten up!

If you're doing the best you can, that's good enough. I don't know many women who aren't doing their absolute level best in every way, but plenty of those women keep track only of the things they *don't* do perfectly. The women I know accomplish a phenomenal amount, but often they don't pay attention to what they've done. Rather they concentrate on what has been left undone or what remains still to do.

I frequently meet women who feel their lives are out of control on some level, women who feel profoundly unhappy, women who are trying their hardest but who still feel that somehow it isn't enough or that they haven't done it right or that they aren't acceptable to the Lord the way they are. And sometimes, women hear messages coming from their own sisters in the gospel and the organization of the Church that reinforce these feelings of sadness and inadequacy. This hurts me. This is not the gospel. It's not what the Church is for.

"Lighten up" isn't a message that implies, "Be irresponsible." It's a message for women who are already taking their responsibilities so seriously that they feel burdened and weighed down by them. Remember that lovely promise from the Savior in Matthew 11:28–30: "Come unto me, all ye that labour and are heavy laden, and I will give you rest. Take my yoke upon you, and learn of me; for I am meek and lowly in heart: and ye shall find rest unto your souls. For my yoke is easy, and my burden is light."

How can the burden be light? It's because the yoke is a double one, designed for two. Jesus wants to be our yokefellow; yet how often do we struggle on, insisting on pulling the whole load ourselves, never realizing why it feels so lopsided? The Savior wants to share that burden, and we need to let him.

So just memorize that ancient proverb and say it out loud when things are hard. Lighten up!

You're going to have some dark moments. We all do. But when they come, I hope you will remember to let the sunshine into your life. Don't be hard on yourself, and don't let other people be hard on you either. Give yourself credit for the good things you do. If you make a mistake, give yourself credit for trying. Laugh a lot. Catch yourself singing. Whistle or hum as you go about your duties. If you do only half of what you wanted to do, or do it only half as well as you would have liked, pat yourself on half your back. But lighten up! Be lighthearted enough that you can float above the dark clouds and see the rainbows in your life. The gospel brings a whole rainbow of light into our lives. There are three ideas about this diversity that I'd like to discuss: knowing, helping, and loving. I've borrowed these ideas from the happiest little song about diversity that I know: "We Are Different," by Patricia Kelsey Graham (*Children's Songbook* [Salt Lake City: The Church of Jesus Christ of Latter-day Saints, 1989], p. 263).

> *I know you, and you know me.*
> *We are as diff'rent as the sun and the sea.*
> *I know you, and you know me,*
> *And that's the way it is supposed to be.*
>
> *I help you, and you help me.*
> *We learn from problems, and we're starting to see.*
> *I help you, and you help me,*
> *And that's the way it is supposed to be.*
>
> *I love you, and you love me.*

*We reach together for the best we can be.*
*I love you, and you love me,*
*And that's the way it is supposed to be.*

KNOWING EACH OTHER

For most of my life, I have had to build bridges intercul-
turally. I remember very clearly the point at which I made the
choice to be a bridge builder. On December 7, 1941, the day
the Japanese Imperial Air Force destroyed the American fleet at
Pearl Harbor, I was fifteen years old. When we saw the planes
and heard the bombs, we didn't know if a landing party was
on its way, if the Americans would retaliate, or which side
might pose the most danger to us as Japanese-Americans.

My mother and I were terrified. We gathered everything in
the house that had come from Japan and stuffed it into the
incinerator. We burned fans, books, documents, pictures —
anything that might say, "A Japanese family lives here." When
we were through, I looked in the mirror, saw my face, and
thought, I *am* Japanese. I have never set foot in Japan. I am
not Japanese in my heart. If a Japanese submarine landed on
our beach and Japanese soldiers came ashore, I would run away
from them. But I cannot run away from myself. My eyes, my
skin, and my hair are Japanese. I will always be Japanese."

That realization cut through my confusion and fear. I realized then that there was no easy answer. I realized that many
things might happen over which my family and I would have
no control. But no matter what happened, I would have to deal
with reality — and that involved being both Japanese and American. I would have to work out the answer to who I was a day
at a time, doing the best that I could. Either I would build a
bridge between the two cultures, finding a way to accept both
parts of myself, or else I would remain forever lost between
the two worlds.

So, Ed and I were Japanese in our ancestry, Hawaiian by place of birth, and mainland American by place of residence. (We lived in Utah or Colorado nearly all of our married life.) When we went to Japan on our mission, we may have looked Japanese, but the members would tell you that we seemed very American in what we did. So we had claims on three cultures, but did not totally belong in any one of the three. It was our task to build bridges between these cultures, or else we would have been isolated, stranded between worlds, belonging to none of them.

The greatest bridge of all is the culture of the gospel. "For by one Spirit are we all baptized into one body," Paul wrote to the Corinthians, "whether we be Jews or Gentiles [or Cambodians or Japanese or blacks or Bolivians], whether we be bond or free; and have been all made to drink into one Spirit." (1 Corinthians 12:13.)

Perhaps because I have been part of three cultures, without totally belonging to any of the three, I can see that there are things in every culture that we must give up in order to truly enter into the culture of the gospel. This is a culture based on the atonement of Christ and the restoration of his pure gospel through the Prophet Joseph Smith. Faith, repentance, baptism, the gift of the Holy Ghost, living together in a righteous community, and serving each other with love are all principles of that culture. These principles are true in any culture and among all peoples. We all must be baptized, whether we wear sandals or cowboy boots or go barefoot. We must find ways to serve, whether that involves caring for a child with spina bifida, working with integrity and care to create a piece of furniture, or running for public office.

To make our diversity a strength, not a divisiveness, we need to communicate more and communicate better. As sisters in the gospel, let's talk. Let's share experiences. When we see or

8

hear something we don't understand, let's check it out. Let's ask, "Can you tell me what it means when you say or do this?"

HELPING EACH OTHER

Once we stop looking at our differences as barriers, it becomes easier to reach across them to help each other. As the daughter of a Japanese plantation laborer, I knew clearly that there was a social barrier between us and the *haoles*, or Caucasians, that was hard to cross—but helping was one way to do so.

Captain Beck, who managed the plantation, was at the pinnacle of society in our village. He was the most important person around. I had a reputation for being quick and skillful, so from the time I was nine or ten, his Japanese cook hired me to help serve at parties. The pay wasn't extravagant—twenty-five or fifty cents—but I probably would have gone for nothing just to see the *haole* way of doing things.

I watched everything! How *haoles* talked to each other, how they drank cocktails, how they sat down and stood up (chairs weren't a usual part of Japanese furniture), what they ate, and how they manipulated those strange, awkward implements called forks. Then I came back to my own home with my mind whirling with all these differences. I never thought, "The *haole* way must be better because Captain Beck is more important than my parents." Instead, I thought, "So the *haole* way is different in all of these ways that I have seen." And I stored them away.

Because I was willing to be a servant—because I was willing to help—I learned things about the world I lived in that I could not have otherwise discovered for many years. Just as Patricia's song says, "I help you, and you help me."

A second way in which this mysterious Captain Beck and I helped each other was at the annual Christmas pageant. Every

9

year he sponsored a Christmas party for the plantation workers. There was a nativity play, the singing of Christmas carols (can you imagine the thrilling, sweet harmonies of the Hawaiians as they sang about a little town called Bethlehem?), and wonderful presents from a terrifying fat man in a red suit and a white beard. I didn't understand any of it; but when Captain Beck asked me to be the angel in the nativity play, I was proud to be chosen and I worked hard to memorize my part.

"Fear not," I said. "For, behold, I bring you good tidings of great joy." I didn't know what shepherds were or why they were afraid or what good tidings were. I was just a skinny eight-year-old in a white sheet costume with crooked tinsel wings and a scratchy tinsel halo on my head. But later, when I became acquainted with the Church and realized that the baby was Jesus, the good tidings of the gospel became real to me. If I had refused to help, I might have felt differently about those good tidings of joy.

You might not think your help is significant, but Mother Teresa feels differently. She says, "I always say I'm a little pencil in the hands of God. He does the thinking. He does the writing. He does everything — and it's really hard — sometimes it's a broken pencil. He has to sharpen it a little more. But be a broken instrument in His hands so that He can use you anytime, anywhere. . . . We have only to say Yes to Him." (As quoted in *Women and the Power Within* [Salt Lake City: Deseret Book, 1990], pp. 33–34.) Louise Y. Robison, general president of the Relief Society from 1928 to 1939, urged us to "welcome the tasks that make you go beyond your ordinary self, if you would grow."

Isn't that what the song means? "We learn from problems, and we're starting to see." What is it that we start to see? We see that our differences are great strengths to us.

LOVING EACH OTHER

The third verse of the song says: "I love you, and you love me./We reach together for the best we can be." Knowing, serving, and loving—they're all mixed together. We can't serve others if we don't know their needs. We learn to love by serving. Don't be afraid to be the first to reach out, to offer to help, to extend sincere love. It can be difficult and even frightening at times. It's always hard being the first one to do anything, but it's important to keep doors open.

All our lives Ed and I have been pioneers, out there on a culture frontier. In the early 1950s, when we moved to Salt Lake City, it had not been long since World War II, and many Salt Lake families had lost loved ones in the Pacific Theater. People on the street did not know we were Americans from Hawaii. They saw our Japaneseness and sometimes responded out of feelings left over from the war. They did not know that Ed had voluntarily enlisted with the 442nd Infantry, a Japanese-Hawaiian unit of legendary bravery that became the most decorated unit in the U.S. Army. He had risked his life to defend the United States and had been so severely wounded in France that his recuperation had taken another year of his life. So although the racist comments we occasionally heard were unfair—as racist comments always are—we did not resent them. We simply tried to make each interaction we had with any individual one that would give that person a different feeling about us in particular and about Japanese people in general.

We first rented an apartment in the Bonneville Ward, where Ted Jacobsen was bishop. The welcome he and his wife, Florence, gave us was wonderful. We were promptly called to serve in the ward and had many opportunities to interact with other members, which we appreciated.

After Ed graduated with his master's degree and we were in a position to buy a home, our bishop tried to keep us in the ward, but no lots were available for sale. We followed real estate ads closely and telephoned agents when we saw a home advertised for sale somewhere close to our neighborhood, for I wanted to live near the elementary school where I was teaching, and Ed hoped for a reasonably short drive to the Veterans' Administration Hospital.

Nearly always the same thing happened. When the realtor heard our name, there would be a long moment of silence, and then he or she would say something like, "I'm afraid that house is no longer on the market, but could I interest you in a home somewhere else?" The realtor would then name one of Salt Lake City's ethnic neighborhoods.

One contractor friend, Ken Biesinger, who heard about our difficulties, said, "I'll build a home for you in the development where I'm working now." It was further away from downtown than we had hoped, but we were pleased with the prospect and eagerly made the down payment on the lot. In a few days our friend gave us back the deposit. "There's a 'gentleman's agreement' not to sell to Japanese people," he said. He was embarrassed and angry, and we were hurt; but we were certainly not upset at him.

Then love intervened. Ed was then serving a regional mission among the Japanese in Salt Lake City, and his companion, Grant Burns, came to our rescue by selling us a lot he owned. Finally we were able to build a home. When the house was nearly finished and it was time for us to move in, Ed and I decided it would be a good idea for us to make an effort to meet our new neighbors. Leading three-year-old Ken by the hand and carrying two-year-old Bob, we walked up and down the street, ringing each doorbell and introducing ourselves. No one was unfriendly or made any unpleasant remarks, but we could tell there was a certain amount of discomfort. And no one—not one family—invited us to come in and sit down.

We were perhaps a little discouraged, but not dismayed. We knew we had a responsibility to reach out to people, and we did not want to cross the line between being friendly and being pushy. Still, we attended church in our new ward for the first time with a little trepidation. We found a loving welcome from two families: Blair and Lillian Bradshaw, who had lived in Hawaii, and Abe and Nell Sieverts, whose parents were converts from Holland and who, perhaps, had experienced something of our concern about finding ways to be accepted. They knew enough not to be uneasy at our differences. They cared enough to make us welcome.

It was only a matter of time before people got to know us and were able to see beyond our visible differences. We spent ten happy years in that ward feeling completely accepted and valued. I recall a marvelous experience a few years later when Ed was serving as a counselor in the bishopric and I had caught measles from one of the children at school. I was in bed, feeling feverish and uncomfortable, when Ed came home from bishopric meeting and said, "The bishop really chewed me out tonight, and you, too!"

"What's the matter?" I asked.

Ed laughed. "He was upset that we hadn't told him you were sick and that the Relief Society wasn't here helping with the boys and the cooking. He said, 'Your wife is one of the first people in the ward to be there when anyone else needs help, and now she's denying people of the blessing of giving. It's her turn now, and she has to learn how to receive.'"

I certainly did! People were just wonderful, and we have only good memories of that ward.

Love is not just a nice feeling about someone. It is the pure and joyful pulse of the universe, and being in tune with it means you are in tune with the forces that bind together the stars on one hand and the atoms on the other. If we truly love each other, most differences become irrelevant and most forms of helping are pure delight.

Love literally has the power to cause change. During the 1970s, Ohio University conducted an experiment on rabbits, feeding them high-cholesterol diets and hoping to duplicate the effect that such a diet has on human arteries. "Consistent results began to appear in all the rabbit groups except for one, which strangely displayed 60 percent fewer symptoms. Nothing in the rabbits' diet could account for their high tolerance to the diet until it was discovered by accident that the student who was in charge of feeding these particular rabbits liked to fondle and pet them. He would hold each rabbit lovingly for a few minutes before feeding it; astonishingly, this alone seemed to enable the animals to overcome the toxic diet. Repeat experiments, in which one group of rabbits was treated neutrally while the others were loved, came up with similar results." (Deepak Chopra, *Quantum Healing: Exploring the Frontiers of Mind/Body Medicine* [New York: Bantam Books, 1989], p. 33.)

The student could not change the diet or refuse to give the high-cholesterol food. But what he did was to define a new reality for the rabbits. He did not see them primarily as animals that were going to die. Instead, they were worth loving. Because his assignment was to be with them, he was kind and gentle. And somehow, that attention was enough. Something within the rabbit itself seemed to reorganize its body chemistry to resist the toxic diet.

This example calls to mind the Savior's promise: "I am come that they might have life, and that they might have it more abundantly." (John 10:10.) According to the measurements we usually use, for the most part Jesus did not make people's lives physically better. He fed the five thousand and healed the sick and even raised some from the dead, but his whole nation remained in political bondage. He didn't permanently improve anybody's standard of living or assure better jobs or good educations. Can we really say that he gave them a more abundant life?

Yes, he did. The Savior didn't want to give his followers a better version of the old life; he wanted to give them a new life. He gave them transformation, abundance, victory. And he did it by loving them. It is that same love that he feels for us, here and now.

I hope we can accept our differences, rejoice in our differences, and build a strong sisterhood in our differences. When you feel lost, lonely, and marginalized, when you feel you are too different from everyone else in the Church and too insignificant to make a contribution, perhaps you will think of me. I was once a skinny Buddhist girl, speaking pidgin English, wearing crooked tinsel wings and bringing "glad tidings" without understanding them. Since that time I have served in many capacities in the Church. When I was called to the Relief Society general presidency, President Thomas S. Monson said that, to his knowledge, I was the first woman in modern times to have served on the general boards of all three auxiliaries. You, too, have contributions to make. Who knows what the Lord has prepared for you?

So, lighten up! We are the rainbow, but it is Christ who is the light. When John the Beloved was caught away in his vision of the Holy City, he said: "Immediately I was in the spirit: and, behold, a throne was set in heaven, and one sat on the throne. And he that sat was to look upon like a jasper and a sardine stone: and there was a rainbow round about the throne." (Revelation 4:2–3.)

Could we be that rainbow? I think it's possible. We can learn not just to accept but to enjoy each other's differences, and to lighten up when the pressures and challenges loom heavy. In our diversity, we manifest the pure light of Christ. Let us know each other, help each other, and love each other.

CHAPTER TWO

# Principles and Practices

I HAVE A FAVORITE SAYING that summarizes an important concept, particularly as we come to rejoice in each other's uniqueness and in our cumulative diversity:

In principles, great clarity.

In practices, great charity.

That's what I want us to have as Latter-day Saints. I want us all to have real clarity about the principles of the gospel that unite us. I want us to understand to the marrow of our bones that Jesus is the Christ, that his atonement releases us from the bondage of sin and error, that the covenants we make are eternally honored by our Heavenly Father, and that the ordinances of the gospel exist to perfect us as individuals, to purify us as a community, and to prepare us as a people for the second coming of our Lord. I want those principles to lead us the way the pillar of fire by night led the children of Israel in the wilderness. I want them to dominate our mental landscapes as the pillar of the cloud towered over them by day. I want singleness of vision when it comes to principles.

But when it comes to practices, I want kaleidoscopic vision. I want the whole world of options to be at our fingertips so that we can consult our needs and wants when we decide how to apply those principles. I want us to make up our own minds, experiment with one form and abandon it without feeling guilty if we find it doesn't work, listen to what works for other people, find something else, seek the Father's will, find still something else, move into a different season of our lives, and find still something else.

Let me give an example of what I mean. We can all agree that there is one major principle underlying the rules and laws governing how to drive a car. That principle is safety. In the United States, that principle is translated into the practice of driving on the right-hand side of the road. In fact, unless you're on a double-lane highway or a one-way street or in other special circumstances, this practice is a law. But if we were in England, the same principle of safety would be translated into exactly the opposite practice: driving on the *left* side of the road. If we tried to fulfill the principle of safety in England using a United States practice, we would certainly break that principle—and we'd be lucky if that were all we broke! Same principle, but opposite practices.

I don't think we have much problem with principles. Everywhere I go, I feel the intensity of the love women have for the gospel, the strength of their faith in the Savior, and their joy in service. But I *do* sense a lot of tension and discomfort sometimes around the issue of practices. I feel women mistrusting other women, or feeling mistrusted or unacceptable themselves, because they don't fit some list of practices.

This is a wonderful time to be a woman in the United States. Whether people interpret it negatively or positively, the women's movement has nonetheless flung open windows of opportunities on all side. Yet I frequently hear sisters say that when they come to Relief Society they feel the options narrow down to a tiny constriction. Some of us walk out feeling walls all around us, straight up and down, thinking there's only one right way to think, to talk, to dress, to *be*. We're afraid that if we say what we really think, everybody on the row in front of us is going to turn around and give us that "schoolteacher" eye.

Once again, may I suggest an important assignment for all of us: Lighten up! Drop those unrealistic expectations. At the general women's meeting in September 1990, Elaine L. Jack, our Relief Society general president, talked about the "Super-woman" she has wanted to meet for thirty years who does everything and does it all right. Then she said, "We can never accurately take the measure of our lives based on social, economic, ethnic, age, marital, or physical conditions." (*Ensign*, November 1990, p. 89.) And I would add that we should never compare ourselves spiritually to someone else either.

There are wonderful consequences when we are able to sort out the principles that unify us and the practices that give us our diversity. This attitude frees us to celebrate our diversity as sisters. Philosopher Max De Pree describes this as "abandoning ourselves to the strengths of others." (*Leadership Is an Art* [New York: Dell, 1989], p. 9.)

An excellent discussion of principles and practices in the context of Church service is Paul's wonderful letter to the Corinthians. The following modern translation helps me think about the ideas in a new way:

"The body is a unit, though it is made up of many parts; and though all its parts are many, they form one body. So it is with Christ. For we were all baptized by one Spirit into one body—whether Jews or Greeks, slave or free—and we were all given the one Spirit to drink.

"Now the body is not made up of one part but of many. If the foot should say, 'Because I am not a hand, I do not belong to the body,' it would not for that reason cease to be part of the body. And if the ear should say, 'Because I am not an eye, I do not belong to the body,' it would not for that reason cease to be part of the body. If the whole body were an eye, where would the sense of hearing be? If the whole body were an ear, where would the sense of smell be? But in fact God has arranged the parts in the body, every one of them, just as he wanted them to be. If they were all one part, where would the body be? As it is, there are many parts, but one body. The eye cannot say to the hand, 'I don't need you!' And the head cannot say to the feet, 'I don't need you!' On the contrary, those parts of the body that seem to be weaker are indispensable, and the parts that . . . are unpresentable are treated with special modesty, while our presentable parts need no special treatment. But God has combined the members of the body and has given greater honor to the parts that lacked it, so that there should be no division in the body, but that its parts should have equal concern for each other. If one part suffers, every part suffers with it; if one part is honored, every part rejoices with it." (1 Corinthians 12:12–26, New International Version [Grand Rapids, Michigan: Zondervan Bible Publishers, 1978]. Hereafter cited as NIV.)

After developing this marvelous analogy, Paul talks about the different offices and spiritual gifts that different people may be blessed with. Then, to underscore the point that we should all learn from each other, he asks pointedly, "Did the word of God originate with you? Or are you the only people it has reached?" (NIV, 1 Corinthians 14:36.)

Sometimes we think we can't be united unless we're all the same—doing the same things, talking the same way, understanding a gospel idea the same way. I think the Apostle Paul has a very different opinion.

At a regional meeting I attended, one of the stake Relief Society presidents was concerned because the women in one ward were holding an overnight slumber party for homemaking meeting. "Is this all right?" she asked anxiously.

"Are you concerned about their children?" I asked, somewhat puzzled.

"Oh, no. There's no problem with the children. They're taken care of. But are they *supposed* to be doing this?"

"Are they doing it too often, do you think?"

"Oh, no. They don't do it very often."

"Is their bishop supportive?"

"Yes, he has approved the idea," she answered.

Finally I saw the problem: These sisters were doing something different, something nontraditional, something not mentioned in curriculum guidelines. Therefore it must be wrong. I tried to help this Relief Society president think about the principle instead of the practice—and the principle is embodied in the question I asked her: "Is it meeting their needs?"

She blinked at me. "*Their* needs?" She thought for a minute and then replied, "I guess so. They seem to really enjoy it and have a good time. They say it's important to them to have time to talk."

"Well, then," I said encouragingly, "aren't they doing exactly what the handbook says should happen at homemaking meetings? They have selected an activity that meets their needs and have obtained the approval of their priesthood leaders."

If the principle is clear, many practices will help our Relief Society sisterhood thrive: an overnighter in one place, a quilting project in another place. They're both correct practices according to the principle of meeting needs of sisters, but what would be very effective in one ward wouldn't necessarily work in another area. That's why each ward Relief Society presidency ministers differently—and that's great!

You know, you can't have harmony in music if everybody is singing in unison. Think of singing a hymn where there was only soprano—no alto, tenor, or bass. We need all the parts. Think of trying to sing a round without diversity! A round is

21

fun because it's based on the complicated harmonies of singing the same tune at a different time than everyone else. We're all singing the same song – not just making random sounds – and singing the same message, but the music is a lot more beautiful and powerful when we *don't* all sing the same note.

Elder John K. Carmack had a wonderful article published in the March 1991 *Ensign* titled "Unity in Diversity." In it he pointed out the unity that comes from our underlying faith in Christ and the basic practices of the Church, then warned against two barriers to unity: labeling and unfairness. He wrote: "Labeling a fellow Church member an intellectual, a less-active member, a feminist, a South African, an Armenian, a Utah Mormon, or a Mexican, for example, seemingly provides an excuse to mistreat or ignore that person. . . . Each of us should be fair to everyone, especially the victims of discrimination, isolation, and exclusion. Let us be careful not to snicker at jokes that demean and belittle others because of religious, cultural, racial, national, or gender differences. All are alike unto God. We should walk away or face up to the problem when confronted with these common and unworthy practices." (Page 9.)

Hooray for differences! Without them, there would be no harmony. *In principles, great clarity. In practices, great charity.*

Another effect of being able to separate unity in principles from diversity in practices is that it relieves fragmentation and distraction. If we are focused on what the Spirit is telling us about a particular principle, then we are less tormented by the cacophony of today's voices, all giving us different tasks.

In this spirit, consider a question that is sensitive for many Latter-day Saint women: Are you a good Mormon mother? The Church has a real interest in seeing that children are reared according to gospel principles, so it has been very free with instructions, counsel, and prescriptions to its women. For many women, these instructions have been helpful. For others, they have been a source of pain. The principle behind motherhood is that we as women have the great responsibility and the wonderful blessing, ideally in partnership with our husbands, of teaching our children the gospel. Our Heavenly Father entrusts most of us with other precious spirit children who aren't quite as far along as we are in terms of mortal experience. But how are we supposed to teach the gospel effectively to our children? Well, at this point we leave the bumper stickers behind and have whole libraries of books — because practices vary so much!

I have been extremely interested in a book by William G. Dyer and Phillip R. Kunz, both faculty members at Brigham Young University, called *Effective Mormon Families: How They See Themselves.* (Salt Lake City: Deseret Book, 1986.) The authors asked several stake presidents to name the "best" fifteen families in their stakes. They wanted families who had been raising children for a long time, not starry-eyed newlyweds; so the families had to have at least one grown child. But they didn't want people whose children were all gone and for whom the reality of raising children was obscured by nostalgia. So the families had to have at least one teenager still at home. They surveyed over three hundred families and based their final conclusions on about two hundred usable surveys, which they supplemented with interviews.

A lot of what they found is about what you'd guess: 99 percent of these families always paid their tithing; 93 percent said they always accepted Church callings; nearly all of them were sealed in the temple; and for 99 percent of them, temple marriage for the children was a family goal. But there were also a lot of variations in practices. When the interviewers asked if they usually had family prayer, 73 percent of them said yes; 66 percent usually held family home evening; 24 percent went to the temple regularly, and 28 percent had regular family scripture study. (See pages 17–21.) Of course, there are individual circumstances that lie behind these statistics. Many people lived far from a temple. Many families with teenagers were trying to juggle the work schedules of three, four, or five people simultaneously. Many of the programs that we think are absolute "musts" for righteous families are very recent, while most of these families established their traditions and patterns early in the family cycle—fifteen or twenty years ago. But what does this tell us about principles and practices? Obviously, there's a lot of clarity on principles, and lots of leeway on practices. Yet all of these families were, in the opinion of their stake presidents, effective and successful. Isn't that encouraging?

One of the authors' most exciting discoveries for me was this: "You don't have to come from a strong LDS family yourself to have one. Forty-nine percent of the husbands and 39 percent of the wives had not graduated from seminary. Only 21 percent of the husbands had been on missions. Twenty percent of the fathers and 18 percent of the mothers were not baptized at age eight. Between 15 and 18 percent were baptized after the age of twelve." (Page 14.)

What made the difference? "We asked a cluster of questions trying to find out where this commitment to the Church came from and were impressed to discover, once again, the principle of agency. Commitment did not just happen, and it wasn't just programmed into parents by their own parents. It was a conscious decision. . . . At some point, sometimes before marriage, sometimes as a couple, these people decided that their own children would be raised up in a gospel environment. . . . [And] they followed it up with action." (Page 14.)

I liked what I read. Ed and I are both converts. We had to decide on our own what kind of Mormons we were going to be and what kind of Latter-day Saint home we would establish. We listened to a lot of counsel. We observed a lot of families. But we still had to make our own decisions.

What's the principle? Teach your children the gospel. And what's the practice? That depends on your needs and wants and your family's needs and wants. Should you have one child or eight? Should you have cookies on the counter every day after school? Should you unplug the TV set? Should you never spank? Should you sometimes spank?

It depends. These are practices, options based upon needs. You get to choose what works for you and your family. So lighten up! Lighten up about yourself—and about other people.

Brother Dyer and Brother Kunz had a comment about guilt that I want to share with you: "Many couples still feel somewhat apologetic or guilty because, although they are carrying out a Church program, they are not doing it the 'Church way' and feel that their families would work even better if somehow they could do it 'by the book.' They genuinely want to do everything the Church teaches them to do, and they want to do it perfectly. Yet in these effective families, they do not feel paralyzed by the desire for perfection. The statistics and interviews paint a remarkable picture of being simultaneously contented with family strengths while never feeling they can say, 'We've got it made.' " (Page 17.)

Isn't that great! What a wonderful way of continuing to work toward perfection without berating yourself for not being perfect yet. I love the way one former general president of the Relief Society, Barbara Smith, expressed it: "Ideals are stars to steer by. They are not a stick to beat ourselves with."

If we focus on principles instead of practices, we free ourselves from the unwarranted and unnecessary burden of guilt that often ensues when our practices do not match those of everyone else. We also free ourselves from the even more terrible burden of judging others because their practices don't match ours. A focus on principles leaves us free to deal with the essentials instead of feeling fragmented by competing demands and tasks. And a focus on principles lets us rejoice in our diversity.

Does all this mean that anything goes, that there are no rules? Of course not. We lighten up so that we can approach heaven, not so that we drift along like the clouds Jude talked about: "Clouds they are without water, carried about of winds; trees whose fruit withereth, without fruit, twice dead, plucked up by the roots; raging waves of the sea, foaming out their own shame; wandering stars, to whom is reserved the blackness of darkness for ever." (Jude 1:12–13.)

Sister Jutta Baum Busche, the wife of Elder F. Enzio Busche, gave a wonderful description of the balance we need to keep our feet on the ground and our faces toward heaven: "The one great stumbling block to our progress in faith is rule-keeping that does not spring from an honest heart. Too many people imply in their attitude toward others that our Heavenly Father expects perfect conformity to established rules. But Jesus Christ never condemned the honest in heart. His wrath was kindled against the hypocritically empty rule-keeping of the Pharisees." ("The Unknown Treasure," in *Women and the Power Within: To See Life Steadily and See It Whole*, Dawn Hall Anderson and Marie Cornwall, eds. [Salt Lake City: Deseret Book, 1991], p. 23.)

There is great peace in righteous principles and great strength in a diversity of righteous practices. Louise W. Madsen, a former counselor in the general Relief Society presidency, said: "The [Relief] Society as a whole . . . receiv[es] power from God by 'union of feeling,' which best serves to do the work which the Lord would have done by an organization of his daughters." Her colleague, Marianne Clark Sharp, added, "The power of

Relief Society is the sum of the individual members' testi-monies—humble, burning testimonies which burn away dis-harmony, bickering, or ill feelings and engender a spirit of unity and the building up of each other." (*Relief Society Magazine*, 1962, p. 805.)

Of course we must be united in principle. We must share the humble, burning testimonies that Sister Sharp describes. We must find ways to pray together, to bear testimony together, to share the ways in which the Savior touches and blesses our lives. If I know how you feel about Jesus Christ, I am much less worried with how you feel about many other things. Your practices may be a rainbow of diversity—violet, blue, green, yellow, orange, and red. But behind this diversity of color, I will see the Savior's pure, white light, shining steadily.

# CHAPTER THREE

# Walk in My Zori

THERE IS A SAYING IN THE American West about walking in the other person's moccasins. Well, in Hawaii we have Japanese slippers called *zori* instead. These slippers are very special to me, because my life literally would not have been the same except for many pairs of *zori*.

My parents had little education themselves. Mother loved school but had to drop out in the sixth grade to care for her two younger sisters after her mother died. My parents wanted me to get an education so that I could have a better future than being a plantation laborer, as they were.

From the time I was fifteen, I lived away from home, working as a maid to put myself through high school. Then later, when I was going to college in Honolulu, I worked selling jewelry at Sears Roebuck and as a clerk at the Swedish consulate. My burning desire was to become a teacher. My parents helped me with the tuition, but there was never very much money. I had to be careful of every penny. I thought that the money for my tuition came from my father's earnings, and it was only after I had graduated from college that I learned differently. My family earned my tuition fifty cents at a time by making *zori*.

Think of it. Each week, a contractor would bring a huge pile of *lauhala* leaves to our village and pick up the finished *zori*, which were sold all over the islands, or maybe in the Far East, and in import-export stores. The *lauhala* leaves are long, with

29

a row of spines running down each edge, and very fibrous. My two little brothers, Hiro and Tsugio, would prepare the leaves by scraping off the spines. I'm sure there were many times when their fingers would bleed from being torn by the thorns. Then they would scrape the fleshy part of the leaf away, leaving only the flat, fibrous part, soak this in water to make it pliable, and then roll it up into a little bundle to be stored until my parents could work on it. My father would slice the leaves with his sharp razors and weave the strips into the *zori* fabric. My mother would sew the fabric on her little foot-powered treadle sewing machine to a pattern form, trim the top edge and roll it over and sew it so that it wouldn't unravel, and then sew it to the fabric sole to finish the *zori*. My tuition was about three hundred dollars per semester, so at fifty cents a pair that meant my family would have to make six hundred pairs of *zori* every three or four months.

Whenever I went home for vacations, I always helped with the *zori*. Everyone in our little village was poor and anxious to do any kind of piece work they could, and I just thought this was part of our family's work. I did not realize that this was the sacrifice of my whole family for my education.

Every time I see these *zori*, I think of my family sustaining me so that I could walk forward into my future. And I appreciate that sacrifice. In how many Oriental families would such a sacrifice have been made for the education of a daughter?

I have wondered sometimes why my parents did not tell me that these *zori* were for my education. Perhaps they thought that the burden of obligation would be too heavy for me. But also, it is not the Japanese way to acknowledge either achievement or obligation directly. Whenever anyone praised me as a child, I knew that my mother was very proud of me, though she always said, "Oh, she has much to learn."

Whenever anyone gave us a gift — and our Japanese and Hawaiian neighbors were always generous with what little they had — my mother taught me to return the plate, clean and polished, and bear another gift in return. The size of the gift was not important. She would say, "We must return something, if only a box of matches." Little boxes of wooden matches sold for a penny when I was a girl. It was not a feeling of paying something back in kind, in the sense of purchasing a service or giving someone a wage. Instead, it was a recognition of a reciprocal relationship of giving and taking. I remember my mother would say, "*On gaeshi.*" Those words do not mean "Be grateful," or "Return the favor," but rather, "Acknowledge the obligation," with even a little sense of "*Honor* the obligation." When I first read the Book of Mormon, I understood this feeling of "*on gaeshi*" when I read King Benjamin's sermon:

"For behold, are we not all beggars? Do we not all depend upon the same Being, even God, for all the substance which we have, for both food and raiment, and for gold, and for silver, and for all the riches which we have of every kind?

"And behold, even at this time, ye have been calling on his name, and begging for a remission of your sins. And has he suffered that ye have begged in vain? Nay; he has poured out his Spirit upon you, and has caused that your hearts should be filled with joy, and has caused that your mouths should be stopped that ye could not find utterance, so exceedingly great was your joy." (Mosiah 4:19–20.)

Many of us know that someone has made *zori* for us at fifty cents a pair. We attend schools we did not build. We read books we did not print. We wear clothes that someone else sewed for us. We eat food that someone else grew for us. Many times, we spend money that we did not earn personally. We learn the gospel from teachers who have prepared themselves for our sake. It is a sign of spiritual maturity, I think, to acknowledge that our acceptance of these gifts brings an obligation upon us. There are people to whom we should express appreciation for sacrifices. There are reverent ways in which we should use natural resources, consider the contributions of others, honor those who have gone before.

To acknowledge our dependence, our debt, our relationship to God and to one another does not make us powerless or weak. Rather, it is a relationship of great joy, as King Benjamin has described, of appreciation for the sacrifice, of love, and of gratitude. Whatever we can return is not payment for that sacrifice, but rather a joyful acknowledgment of our relationship and the ties that bind us together.

In the Doctrine and Covenants, there is a sobering verse: "And in nothing doth man offend God, or against none is his wrath kindled, save those who confess not his hand in all things, and obey not his commandments." (D&C 59:21.)

We cannot repay God for his blessings. We cannot purchase his blessings by our service and obedience. He cannot be placed under contract to us. What he wants from us is this acknowledgment of which I have spoken—that we see our relationship to him, that we acknowledge the ties that bind us to him, and that we accept his generous gifts with a loving heart and "confess . . . his hand in all things."

So, the first lesson of the *zori* is an acknowledgment of our obligation. The second lesson is one of order. The *zori* are easy to put on, but only if they are put on one at a time. Think about trying to put them on both at the same time. I imagine you would have to put them down and try to jump into them, and probably miss one or crush the back of one or both. This seems obvious, but it is important. The lesson for me is also a lesson that King Benjamin teaches us: "See that all these things are done in wisdom and order; for it is not requisite that [we] should run faster than [we have] strength." (Mosiah 4:27.)

What is the order of your life right now? Perhaps you are a student. Perhaps you are a young parent, exploring the delights and realizing some of the responsibilities of parenthood. Possibly you have obligations to your employer. Perhaps you are well established in your career and have the opportunity to branch out into community service. This may be a time when a heavy Church responsibility has come to you. Perhaps you are a missionary. Whatever your season is, enjoy it. Don't try to concentrate on the tasks of another season, or cram too many seasons together. Put on your *zori* firmly, freely, confidently, and joyously. Don't stumble or crush the *zori* by trying to do too many life tasks at once.

A mission is an important step; and it is the wisdom of our leaders that, when it comes, it is a full-time assignment that deserves and receives the missionary's complete concentration. Consider the wisdom of that decision by our priesthood leaders as other seasons present themselves. What seasons can and should be combined? What seasons should receive our full attention, if only for a short period? Take delight in the tasks and joys of each season. Be excited and wrapped up and thrilled in the discoveries that come only with your season.

I will never forget when I discovered snow. I was an exchange teacher in Salt Lake City while Ed was working on his master's degree at the University of Utah before either of our sons was born. I was twenty-five years old and had never been out of Hawaii before, so I had never seen snow. I had read about it, of course, but I had not discovered snow. On the first afternoon snow began to fall, I stood at the window of my second-grade classroom and stared. All of those seven-year-olds had seen snow many times, and they wondered that I was so impressed with the snow. They had forgotten their own discovery of snow, because it had occurred when they were babies. I told them, "I have never seen snow. I have to learn about snow. I have to learn how snow falls. Ah, I see that it falls like rain except that it falls very slowly. And it is so white. And silent. It falls without making a sound—no splashing. And the flakes turn around as they fall. I have heard that every flake has six points but that every flake is different. Can this be true?"

I gave each one of them a piece of black paper, and we went outside to catch snowflakes and look at their shapes before they melted. The children had never caught snowflakes on black paper before, and they discovered snow all over again, crying joyously, "See mine!" "Look at this one!" "This one must be two clumped together. Look at how it shines!" We were all taking delight together in the discoveries of the winter season.

What is your season? What are its special challenges, its unique knowledge, its delightful rewards? Rejoice in them. Do not worry that they are different from the discoveries of another season or from someone else's season. Do things in order. Meet this season of your life wholeheartedly.

The third lesson of the *zori* is partnership. It is also obvious. We walk best when each foot takes a turn being in front. If both feet try to be first, yes, it is possible to move forward—but jumping is much more tiring than walking. This is the lesson of rhythm in life that moves the body forward. I want to compare this to the sharing and partnership that a husband and wife must have to move the family forward.

One summer when Ed and I were vacationing in Hawaii, we went jogging on a lovely track that went around a lagoon of blue water with beautiful trees shading the track. Great vines looped down, and sweet-scented flowers were blooming every-where. We each had different training programs we were working on; as we jogged and ran and walked, now one of us would go faster and now the other one would. At one point, we were exactly opposite each other across the lagoon. I remember look-ing across at Ed in his blue shorts and thinking, "If anyone looked at us, I wonder who they would think is ahead. Who is leading whom?"

It was a silly question, of course. We were both just doing our job the best way we could. Our marriage was like that — a team effort — and it might not have worked so well if we had spent much time thinking about who the leader was. Instead, we concentrated on our tasks. We never asked, "Who is more important? Who should be doing this job? Who should be giving instructions?" Instead, we always asked ourselves, "*What* is this job that needs to be done? Who can do it best? What is best for the job? What is best for the family?" For many couples a traditional division of tasks is good, but it would not have worked well for us. We were not a traditional couple, so we did not choose a traditional way — and I think that's one of the reasons we were such a good team.

Throughout most of our marriage both of us were working every day, coming home every evening, taking care of our chil-dren together, and sharing our work lives — Ed his experiences as a social worker, I my experiences in the classroom. We always worked together to feed the children, clean up the kitchen, help with homework, vacuum the living room, and fold the socks. A sinkful of dishes doesn't care whether the person who washes them is a man, a woman, or a child. They just need to be washed. And most tasks are that way.

The 1990s are a time of transition for American families, and transitions are always confusing. There are many voices telling you what kind of relationship you should have with your husband or wife, what kind of a parent you need to be, what kinds of experiences your children need to have. Listen carefully to these messages and ask yourself, "Will this help us be a good team? What is best for us as a couple? What is best for us as a family?" Do not try to fit your life into someone else's idea of what you should be. Be wise and prayerful—and be yourself. Find your own rhythm. It is teamwork—the rhythm of each foot taking its turn being first—that moves the body forward.

The fourth lesson of the *zori* is the lesson of reciprocity. Each foot, in addition to taking its turn leading out, must also take its turn bearing most of the weight. Just as little progress can be made if one foot always wants to be first, only hopping progress can be made if only one foot bears the body's weight all of the time. This is the lesson of reciprocity, of giving and taking.

We must give and take in every area of life—in marriage, in education, in accepting the sacrifices of others and then, in turn, sacrificing for others—but I want to apply this idea particularly to giving and receiving Church service.

One very busy season of giving for me came when we were living in Littleton Eighth Ward near Denver. Our school district was opening Sunrise Elementary School—a brand-new, year-round, four-track school—and I had been selected to be principal of this school. Organizing the program, hiring the faculty, preparing the building, and working out the scheduling problems were tasks so great that the school district gave me six months—between January and June when the school would open on its twelve-month schedule—to prepare things. I had a trailer on the construction site where my secretary and I worked. I had my own hard hat to wear out on the site where I inspected the progress every day. I put in full days, every day.

Then the bishop asked to see me and Ed. I had been teaching Sunday School and assumed that I would be receiving a new teaching assignment. Instead he said, "I have had a very difficult time deciding to make this calling, knowing how busy you are. But we are changing the Relief Society presidency, and I have been inspired to call you as president."

My mouth dropped open. I was absolutely stunned. I looked at Ed. He took my hand but his face told me, "Hey, you've got to decide this one for yourself."

I finally gasped, "Bishop, you've got to be kidding!"

He laughed and said, "That's what I told the Lord. Several times. But your name always came right back." He leaned forward and said seriously, "I know how much a Relief Society president can do and how much a Relief Society president wants to do. I know how much else you have to do. I don't want you to teach the sisters to make plastic grapes or bake bread. I want you to build their spirituality."

I looked at Ed again. Ed said, "Chieko, I'll support you in whatever decision you make."

I accepted the calling. I chose my counselors carefully, as I knew that I was going to have to rely on them a great deal. One was also employed full-time. We counted on the sisters to help run the Relief Society and on the visiting teachers to do their job. I delegated many things. I was limited in how much visiting I could do, so I concentrated on the Sunday meetings, on being spiritually prepared myself and greeting the sisters and giving them a short message that would increase their spirituality. Often, I could not remember what I said, but sisters would find me in the hall, or call, or send me a note, thanking me for my words. I planned ahead and stocked the freezer with loaves of banana bread to take to the sisters who I felt really needed a visit from the president.

Ed arranged his schedule so that he could drive me to make night visits, always listened to me discuss how things were going, made good suggestions, and bolstered my confidence. When we had a ward dinner, he was there, putting up the tables, carrying the pans in the kitchen, and complimenting the women on their cooking. The bishop made the calling to one, but he got two. Ed was my partner in everything.

When I was released after two years, the sisters gave me a little autograph book in which they had each written a thought. Ninety-eight percent of the statements mentioned spirituality as important, the new sense they had of themselves, a new confidence in God, a new closeness to each other.

And things went beautifully at school. On the first day, I stood in the main hall and watched the children stream in. The building was beautiful. The teachers were so well organized and prepared that there was not a single lost or confused child. In ten minutes, everyone was in a classroom and activities were under way. I had had a dream of standing in that exact spot and seeing things going just so. On the first day of school, I saw that dream realized.

Then came my season of receiving. In 1973, I was diagnosed as having breast cancer and underwent a radical mastectomy followed by radiation therapy. There was so much that I had to leave to the Lord. I knew that I must not let this time of physical weakness become a time of spiritual weakness as well. I learned to accept each day, just as it came, and to find joy in whatever moments it brought me.

And one of the most important lessons I learned was how to receive. Reciprocity. It was my turn to receive. Louise Erickson, counselor in the Relief Society presidency, knew just how to help me. She drove me every day to the radiation therapy, called me on the phone, and made sure that I did not worry about household things.

Many times when people help us, we have no way to return our thanks directly and must be contented with helping someone else in need. But Louise understood how important it was to me to give, even while I was receiving so very much from her. She was making a pretty afghan out of squares hooked on a small frame. Crocheting is not exactly a Japanese art, but she patiently taught me how to do the pattern. It was a simple pattern, so that in just a half hour I could make a square. How I enjoyed that! When I didn't feel like getting out of bed and even felt too weak to concentrate on reading, I could still make a square and enjoy that little achievement. What a great friend Louise was! She not only gave me the essential service that my body needed while it healed, but she gave me the service that my soul needed as well.

These are the four lessons of the *zori* that I have learned from my own experience. One: the lesson of *"on gaeshi,"* of acknowledging our mutual obligations to each other. Two: the lesson of putting on one *zori* at a time — the lesson of relishing each season of life in turn without trying to rush through them all. Three: the lesson of rhythm — of knowing that progress comes by teamwork and by each person in a marriage taking turns. And four: the lesson of reciprocity — of accepting that there is a time to bear heavy responsibilities and a time to let those responsibilities shift to someone else.

I have learned these lessons by experience — sometimes sorrowful and painful experience, but always, ultimately, joyful experience. I am still learning. I am still a student. I hope I always will be. As I learn and experience all of what this life holds for me, I hope I'll get closer to what the Savior wants me to learn. My great task in this life is the task the Savior has given all of us: "Learn of me." He says this repeatedly in the Doctrine and Covenants: "Learn of me, and listen to my words; walk in the meekness of my Spirit, and you shall have peace in me. I am Jesus Christ." (D&C 19:23–24.) "Declare my gospel and learn of me, and be meek and lowly of heart." (D&C 32:1.) "Hearken . . . and give ear to my word and learn of me what I will concerning you." (D&C 58:1.)

39

My heart is filled with gratitude as I think of my *zori*: of my father's fingers, roughened by his work, smoothing the strips of the dried *lauhala*, of my mother's fingers patiently turning and turning the woven leaves beneath her needle, of my little brothers, carefully stripping the thorns away from the leaves. And I think of the Savior, his hands and feet pierced and bleeding, for me, for you. May we learn from him the lessons of sacrifice, of appreciation, of service, and of sharing joy one with another as we walk through life in our own *zori*.

CHAPTER FOUR

# Limitations: A Fine Line

As I've indicated previously, I've experienced some limitations in life — being raised in humble circumstances, being a Japanese-American, marrying a nonmember, joining the Church without my parents' consent, being able to have only two children, and so on. What do we do with limitations when they loom in front of us? Perhaps you're familiar with the prayer of Reinhold Niebur, adapted for use by Alcoholics Anonymous and other recovery programs: "God, give us grace to accept with serenity the things that cannot be changed, courage to change the things which should be changed, and the wisdom to distinguish the one from the other."

My parents were poor at a time when many people thought ethnic peoples weren't really capable of significantly bettering themselves. There was nothing I could do about being Japanese. But I could do something about being poor — and that was to get an education that would open other doors for me. It was hard, but that was something I could control. Another important choice that lay within my grasp was seeing the good in the Christian gospel and accepting the message of the LDS missionaries. I could have chosen not to marry Ed. There was no guarantee that he would join the Church. But I'm glad that I made the choice I did.

Many people have choices about the number of children they have. We didn't have much choice about the number, but

41

we had quite a lot of choice about how we would raise those two boys. Did I think, because there were "only two," that they weren't worthy of my best effort? Hardly! Working in my profession, and doing absolutely the best job I knew how to do, were also choices that I made—important choices that have brought me much happiness.

There was nothing I could do about cancer except put myself in the hands of the Lord. Because he chose to spare my life at that time, I continue to have choices, and I try to exercise those choices in healthy ways by eating nutritiously, getting enough exercise, and resting properly.

We waste tremendous energy when we fret about our limitations instead of getting on with those portions of our life that are under our control. Let me share a few ways to maximize this feeling of control.

First, we can realize that our perspective on limitations is limited. Paul pled three times with the Lord to remove what he called "a thorn in the flesh." Rather than remove it, the Lord told him, "My grace is sufficient for thee: for my strength is made perfect in weakness." This experience changed Paul's attitude and he said, "Most gladly therefore will I rather glory in my infirmities, that the power of Christ may rest upon me." (2 Corinthians 12:7–9.)

Second, we can consecrate what we have and what we are to the Lord's work. And that doesn't just mean our money and our talents. It also means things we might not think of. Cathy Stokes, the former Relief Society president of Hyde Park Ward in Chicago, is a convert to the Church. She is also a black woman, and when she joined the Church, she said, "I joined with all of me. And that includes my blackness. If the Lord can use my blackness, it's His." The first time she went to the temple, she said, "I took my blackness with me, . . . and that was part of what I consecrated."

"She told of the woman who assisted her in the initiatory ordinances, barely able to articulate through her tears, and apologizing at the end because she had not wanted her personal emotions to interfere with Cathy's experience. 'But I've never had the privilege of doing this for a black woman before,' she explained, 'and I'm so grateful.' Cathy reassured her, 'That's all right. That's one of the things I can do for you that no one else in the temple today could do.' " (Lavina Fielding Anderson, "Making the Good Good for Something: A Direction for Mormon Literature," *Dialogue*, Summer 1985, p. 114.)

Now Cathy is an ordinance worker in the Chicago Temple. Her mere presence is a message to people of all races when they come to the temple. She has been featured in several videotapes produced by the Church, speaking not necessarily as a black woman, but simply as a member of the Church. And because her blackness comes with it, there is always a message about cultural diversity.

The covenant of consecration is particularly meaningful to people who have been to the temple, but it is not confined to them alone. Obviously, my Japaneseness is something I consecrate to the Lord along with other talents, abilities, and desires. I was the first woman of any race other than Caucasian to serve on any general board. I felt that I represented people of color from all over the world in that assignment. I'm the first non-Caucasian to serve in the general presidency of any auxiliary. I give that service gladly, and my Japanese ancestry is one of the factors that I offer up willingly in that service.

Is there something you can also consecrate—something that perhaps you never thought the Lord might want? We think of limitations as something to get rid of, and certainly we should not cling voluntarily to any limitation that hinders our spiritual growth. But what about a physical handicap? What does offering deafness or blindness to the Lord make of that handicap?

What about poverty? What about a spiritual gift such as the gift of faith to be healed? What about a discerning heart? What about the desire to minister? What about singleness? What about the circumstances of a divorce? Don't think that the Lord can do without any of your gifts, no matter how you feel about them.

The third point is that we can do our best, no matter where we are, and not just slide by. Magnifying our callings doesn't mean multiplying our tasks. It means reaching a level of excellence that gives us new joy. It feels wonderful to do your best, even if you're the only person who knows you did it.

And only you know the limitations you have to work against to achieve that goal. In my home where I see it every day hangs a beautiful lacquer tray, the gift of the president of the Japan Pearl Association in Kobe. It shows the stages of development of pearls from one month—where the pearl is just about the size of a pinhead—to a pearl of two years, which is about three-eighths of an inch. Pearls are formed when an oyster tries to cover an irritating grain of sand with smooth layers so that the sand will no longer be irritating. They are graded according to size, shape, and color. This tray displays four different colors of pearls: pink, black, silver, and cream. It shows perfectly round pearls, and it also shows baroque pearls, which are fantastically irregular in size and shape. I don't understand what makes one pearl pink and one pearl silver in color. I don't know why one grain of sand will produce a baroque pearl and another a spherical pearl. But what I admire is what each of those oysters has done with that irritating grain of sand—how it has transformed a limitation into a beautiful pearl.

We all have limitations. No matter how rich or righteous or lucky we are, there are always limitations that we bump up against in mortality. Jesus taught that the kingdom of heaven was like a pearl of great price—that we should give up our lesser pearls and purchase that pearl. (See Matthew 13:45–46.) Sometimes we think of ourselves as grains of sand — irritating gravel in the gears of the universe. I think it makes more sense to think of ourselves as pearls in the making — pearls of great price.

The fourth thing we can do is related to the points about consecrating our whole selves to the work and doing our best. And that's to be grateful. Doctrine and Covenants section 59, one of the most joyful passages of all scripture, talks about being "crowned" with blessings, about the joys of keeping the sabbath, about fasting and prayer as "rejoicing and prayer," and about having "a glad heart and a cheerful countenance" for "the fulness of the earth is yours." Why? Because we've deserved it? Because we've earned it? No, because it is our Father's delight to give it to us: "And it *pleaseth* God that he hath given all these things unto [you]; for unto this end were they made to be used, with judgment, not to excess, neither by extortion. And in nothing [do we] offend God, or against none is his wrath kindled, save those who confess not his hand in all things, and obey not his commandments." (D&C 59:20–21; italics added.)

In "all things"? Surely he means just the good things?

No, I think he means *all* things. When we can thank God for trials, tribulations, irritations, and afflictions, something happens to transform them into blessings. The most amazing part of this phenomenon is that you don't even have to think it will work when you pronounce the words. You just have to be willing to say the words and open your heart to the possibility. This principle works on many of the little occurrences of daily life, but I want to illustrate it with a dramatic, once-in-a-lifetime story. Corrie Ten Boom and her sister Betsie were Dutch women and devout Christians who hid Jews in their home during World War II, until the sisters were captured by the Gestapo and imprisoned. When they were transferred to

Ravensbruck, the women's concentration camp, and moved into new quarters, their barracks were crawling with fleas. Corrie and Betsie had always been scrupulously clean and these vermin were abhorrent to them. Corrie tells the story:

"Here! And here's another one!" I wailed. "Betsie, how can we live in such a place!"

"Show us. Show us how." It was said so matter of factly it took me a second to realize she was praying. More and more the distinction between prayer and the rest of life seemed to be vanishing for Betsie.

"Corrie!" she said excitedly. "He's given us the answer! Before we asked, as He always does! In the Bible this morning. Where was it? Read that part again!"

I glanced down the long dim aisle to make sure no guard was in sight, then drew the Bible from its pouch. . . . "Here it is: 'Comfort the frightened, help the weak, be patient with everyone. See that none of you repays evil for evil, but always seek to do good to one another and to all. . . . Rejoice always, pray constantly, give thanks in all circumstances; for this is the will of God in Christ Jesus—' "

"That's it, Corrie! That's his answer. 'Give thanks in all circumstances!' That's what we can do. We can start right now to thank God for every single thing about this new barracks!"

I stared at her, then around me at the dark, foul-aired room.

"Such as?" I said.

"Such as being assigned here together."

I bit my lip. "Oh yes, Lord Jesus!"

"Such as what you're holding in your hands."

I looked down at the Bible. "Yes! Thank you, dear Lord, that there was no inspection when we entered here! Thank you for all the women, here in this room, who will meet you in these pages."

"Yes," said Betsie, "Thank you for the very crowding here. Since we're packed so close, that many more will hear!" She looked at me expectantly. "Corrie!" she prodded.

"Oh, all right. Thank you for the jammed, crammed, stuffed, packed, suffocating crowds."

"Thank you," Betsie went on serenely, "for the fleas and for—"

The fleas! This was too much. "Betsie, there's no way even God can make me grateful for a flea."

" 'Give thanks in *all* circumstances,' " she quoted. "It doesn't say, 'in pleasant circumstances.' Fleas are part of this place where God has put us."

And so we stood between piers of bunks and gave thanks for fleas. But this time I was sure Betsie was wrong. (Corrie Ten Boom, with John and Elizabeth Sherrill, *The Hiding Place* [New York: Bantam Books, 1971], pp. 197–99.)

But as events turned out, it was Betsie who was right. Both Corrie and Betsie were diligent missionaries, constantly bearing testimony to God, bringing the hope of Christ to women trapped in that dreadful place. Betsie was too sick to go out with the brigades of women workers into the forest where the women had to gather wood. She was assigned to knit stockings for German soldiers; and because there were so many women, Betsie was in a group that had to work in the barracks instead of the work room.

She was a lightning knitter who completed her quota . . . long before noon. She kept our Bible with her and spent hours each [afternoon] reading aloud from it, moving from [sleeping] platform to platform.

One evening I got back to the barracks late. . . . Betsie was waiting for me, as always, so that we could wait through the food line together. Her eyes were twinkling.

"You're looking extraordinarily pleased with yourself," I told her.

"You know we've never understood why we had so much freedom in the big room," she said. "Well—I've found out."

That afternoon, she said, there'd been confusion in her knitting group about sock sizes and they'd asked the supervisor to come and settle it.

"But she wouldn't. She wouldn't step through the door and neither would the guards. And you know why?" Betsie could not keep the triumph from her voice: "Because of the fleas! That's what she said, 'That place is crawling with fleas.'"

My mind rushed back to our first hour in this place. I remembered Betsie's bowed head, remembered her thanks to God for creatures I could see no use for. (*The Hiding Place*, pp. 208–9.)

So Betsie was right after all! Doesn't this give us a different perspective on our own problems and about the power of giving thanks for circumstances that we may consider only handicaps?

These, then, are four points that may be helpful in dealing with our limitations: to recognize how limited our understanding of our limitations may be, to consecrate *all* that we are to our Heavenly Father, to do our best always, and to give thanks in all things.

I remember an experience when all four points were demonstrated to me. When we moved to Utah, I was the first exchange teacher from Hawaii to teach at Uintah Elementary School in Salt Lake City. I had taught elementary school for three years in Hawaii and loved it thoroughly. I knew I could be a successful teacher. But still, I felt twinges of apprehension. It had not been all that long since the end of World War II, and I was braced for some racism.

I was not surprised, then, when my principal called me into the office a few days before school started. Her face told me instantly that something was wrong. Hesitantly she said, "I'm very sorry to say that three of the mothers of students assigned to your second grade have requested that they be transferred to a different room. They don't want their children to have a Japanese teacher."

"Oh, no problem!" I said cheerfully. "Don't worry about it. It's fine with me to make the switch. I will love whoever comes into my class." She looked at me in amazement, then breathed a sigh of relief. When I told Ed about the incident that night, I laughed and said, "Three out of thirty-five isn't bad! I have thirty-two students who want me, and three more who are going to have that chance."

Then I poured all my efforts into making that first day a success. In those days of limited and expensive travel, Hawaii was exotic; and I was Japanese-American from Hawaii, which made me exotic, too. I resolved to *be* exotic. I made a fuschia-colored dress that showed off my skin and black hair and tucked a fuschia flower in my hair. I was the most vivid thing in the whole school that first day.

The custom was for each teacher to meet her children on the playground, call the roll so that each child would know where to come, and lead her children into the classroom. The other two second-grade teachers, as a courtesy to me, said, "Would you like to assemble your class first?" I was absolutely delighted. It was exactly what I had hoped for.

I knew there was a lot of curiosity about me, because many of the second-grade mothers were there with their children. It could have been a threatening situation. I could have chosen to feel frightened and let the children and parents feel that. Or I could have chosen to be ultra-stern and rigidly professional by way of covering that up. But what I wanted the children to feel was my own joy and excitement.

I still remember opening the roll book, calling each child's name clearly, looking directly at each child as he or she came into line, smiling, and making some comment. "James Back-man—what a nice name!" (He came and stood before me and said, "My dad is president of the Salt Lake Board of Education.") "Beth Benson—how carefully you've tied your hair ribbons!" (And she said, "My dad is an apostle in the Church!") You can see how I could have felt just a little intimidated. But when I led them off, I could feel their anticipation.

That very afternoon, the principal took me aside, smiling a little. "Chieko," she said, "I just wanted you to know that those three mothers—you know, the ones who wanted their children in the other classrooms?—have come and asked if their children can be transferred back to you. I told them 'opportunity knocks only once.' " She laughed, "Can you imagine how furious the other mothers would be if I tried to talk them into transferring their children *out* of your room?"

My Japaneseness could have been a limitation. In fact, to those three parents initially it was a limitation. But because I was willing to work with it instead of letting it work against me, and because I did the best I could do, it turned into a wonderful experience for all of us.

The Lord is not shocked by, embarrassed about, or angry at our limitations. Instead, he makes a promise of incredible generosity, kindness, and absolutely unequivocal love to all of us: "And if [you] come unto me, I will show unto [you your] weakness. I give unto [you] weakness that [you] may be humble; and my grace is sufficient for all who humble themselves before me; for if [you] humble [yourself] before me, and

50

have faith in me, then will I make weak things become strong."
(Ether 12:27.)

What a glorious promise! In overcoming limitations through the grace of Jesus Christ, our opportunity is to be among the weak things that become strong in the strength of the Lord. Let us claim that promise!

# Defining Ourselves

CHAPTER FIVE

# "For Such a Time As This"

I AM ALWAYS INSPIRED BY THE account of Esther in the Old
Testament. Women tend to play a minor role in the scriptures,
and yet an entire book is devoted to Esther. She didn't live in
ideal circumstances, though she was a queen. She had to endure
the consequences of many decisions made by the men around
her, apparently with limited input from her. She was allowed
no choice in her husband, and he doesn't seem to have had
exactly an impeccable moral character or even a great deal of
wisdom, though he had a generous heart. She was plucked
from her home and installed in the king's house, apparently
without her consent. She was a woman at a time when women
had no public voice and only limited private influence. Her
influence, though she was a queen, had to be shared with literally
dozens of other women in her husband's life. She belonged to
an ethnic minority with actively hostile enemies. Her physical
freedom was limited; she had to stay in the king's house and
could not even see her uncle. And, except for her maids, she
seems to have been alone in her religious practices.

It seems clear from the record that she did not feel powerful
or confident in her position when she learned that Haman had
persuaded the king to issue the infamous order "to destroy,
kill and annihilate all the Jews—young and old, women and
little children—on a single day." (NIV, Esther 3:13.) When
Mordecai sent a message beseeching her to beg the king for

55

mercy, she explained that, unless the king extended the scepter toward her, it was death to approach him without being summoned—and the king had not sent for her for a month. Mordecai sent back a ringing answer: "Do not think that because you are in the king's house you alone of all the Jews will escape. For if you remain silent at this time, relief and deliverance for the Jews will arise from another place, but you and your father's family will perish. And who knows but that you have come to royal position for such a time as this?"

Esther replied: "Go, gather together all the Jews who are in Susa, and fast for me. Do not eat or drink for three days, night or day. I and my maids will fast as you do. When this is done, I will go to the king, even though it is against the law. And if I perish, I perish." (NIV, Esther 4:13–16.)

You know the story. The king extended his scepter toward Esther and she invited him and Haman to a banquet for three nights running. She then revealed Haman's plot to the king, and Haman was hanged on the scaffold he had erected for Mordecai. Finally, the king issued a new edict allowing the Jews to defend themselves. I have some moral qualms about how ferociously the Jews seem to have seized this permission, not only to defend themselves but to strike down "all their enemies with the stroke of the sword" (Esther 9:5), but there's no question that it was a happy ending for Esther.

We, like Esther, have come to our place for such a time as this. We live in the last days, days of "wickedness and vengeance" (Moses 7:60), days when "we wrestle not against flesh and blood, but against principalities, against powers, against the rulers of the darkness of this world, against spiritual wickedness in high places" (Ephesians 6:12). What does this day require of us? This is a day that calls for courage, a day that calls for forgiveness, and a day that calls for ministering, rather than administering.

All throughout the Church I see women of courage. They run for elective office or work for candidates whom they see as bringing integrity to public service. They staff shelters for battered women, collect toys for children in homeless shelters, and serve soup and a kind word in Salvation Army kitchens. They wrestle against ignorance as they serve on school boards, as classroom volunteers, as literacy tutors. They are voices of moral authority in their neighborhoods by teaching children to ask for the flowers they pick and letting teenagers know that they prize respectfulness rather than rudeness, kindness rather than cruelty, and responsibility rather than carelessness. They serve with integrity as attorneys who value justice, as doctors who cherish the ideal of healing, as teachers who inspire learning.

When the time comes — and such times do come for all of us — to take a stand against immorality, injustice, or unethical behavior, women of courage can articulate the sin clearly but maintain compassion and courtesy in dealing with the sinner. Sheer human decency and civility are two of the most important contributions to our community life that women of courage can make.

Latter-day Saint women must become more directly involved in the lives of their communities, but too often we may be naive and self-righteous in how we do it. We transfer our testimony of the truthfulness of the Church to our position on a variety of other issues. For example, we advance a budget decision in PTA with the same fervor as our feelings about Joseph Smith, and then feel as angry and defensive when someone attacks that same budget proposal as if that individual had attacked our faith. We need to learn that disagreement and diversity are valuable elements of our relationships with each other, both in and out of the Church.

Sometimes we think of courage as occurring only in public arenas. The story of Elizabeth Francis Yeates (the mother of Louise Yeates Robison, the seventh general president of the Relief Society) shows a less public view. Elizabeth was an unlikely candidate for unconventional action. She had never lived or worked on her own. Raised in a cultured home in England with many comforts and strict training but no freedom and a limited, "genteel" education, she married at age fifteen. Within a few years she was the mother of four daughters. She matched the Victorian ideal of women as refined, pious, always gentle, and submissive. She did not care for her own religion, she says, but "it was very respectable, at least." However, she was too polite to refuse a Mormon missionary tract when it was offered, and on a rainy afternoon began reading it. Soon she was absorbed in the account of a debate between Elder John Taylor and some French ministers.

"When I had read it all," she wrote, "I said aloud 'praise the Lord. I have found the right way at last.' " She attended a meeting where Joseph Smith's mission was explained. "To say that I was thrilled with joy but feebly expresses my feelings at that time," she continues. "I could see no other way but to repent of my sins and to be baptized. I knew my people would bitterly oppose it when they knew it, and that my former friends would treat me coldly but it was worse than I ever thought."

That one sentence, "It was worse than I ever thought," contains an agony of heartbreak. Her mother forbade her to reenter her childhood home. Her husband told her she must choose between her family and her faith; weeping in anguish, she refused to deny her testimony, and he abandoned her and their four little girls. Elizabeth found work in a woolen mill, laboring with the baby in a basket by the loom, and managed to support them all. Seeing her undefeated, William returned and took all four children to London. Under the law then, there was nothing she could do to stop him or reclaim them.

She did not falter. Her last moment of hesitation had come on the very brink of her baptism when she looked down into the dark river at midnight, December 4, 1855. (The ceremony was performed in secret because of the risk of persecution.) She wrote, "[I] felt as though I could not possibly go in it, But a Voice seemed to say 'There is no other way.' " In faith, she took that step. "It seemed after that," she wrote, "that every thing had changed. The scales had fallen from my eyes, and the gospel plan was glorious, and I covenanted with My heavenly Father that however dark the clouds may be, if friends turned to be foes that by His help I would serve Him. And I have tried in my faltering way to do so." (Lavina Fielding Anderson, "Elizabeth Francis Yeates: Trial by Heartbreak," *Ensign*, July 1979, pp. 62–63.)

This story has a happy ending. Elizabeth reached Utah, married Thomas Yeates, who loved her with all his heart, and had five more children. Two of the children in England died, but seven-year-old Susan ran away from her father when she was eleven, sought refuge with a Mormon family, and eventually was reunited with her mother in Utah. The father took the last daughter to the ends of the earth, he thought – Michigan – but Susan found her years later through a newspaper advertisement. All four daughters were sealed to Elizabeth and Thomas.

This is a day that requires the private courage to see the truth and embrace it as our own and also the public courage to carry out those moral decisions with integrity, courtesy, and civility. But we will see great evils being done, evils that we will sometimes be powerless to prevent. It is also probable that evils will be done to us. We may lose a child when a so-called friend introduces him or her to drugs. No marriage is divorce-proof, even temple sealings. Random violence from sad, sick people and the accidents of carelessness can maim or kill in even the quietest neighborhoods. Sometimes even more painful are the wounds from family members, friends, and fellow members of the Church whom we trust to love and accept us but who may misunderstand us.

So this day we have come to is also a day that requires forgiveness. In this we take our model from the Savior, who on the cross forgave those who inflicted this slow death by torture upon him, saying, "Father, forgive them; for they know not what they do." (Luke 23:34.) He learned forgiveness from our Father in heaven who, as the prophet Nehemiah says, is "a God ready to pardon, gracious and merciful, slow to anger, and of great kindness." (Nehemiah 9:17.)

Forgiveness is not the same thing as pretending that there's nothing to forgive. Great wrongs inspire deep indignation. It does no good to pretend that we are not angry when injustice, cruelty, or sheer stupidity destroys peace and happiness in our families and communities. We should not pretend that something doesn't matter or didn't hurt us when it *does* matter and it *did* hurt.

But we also need to remember that forgiveness is one of the blessings that lies within God's gifts. A dramatic example of this gift comes from the life of Corrie Ten Boom, who survived incarceration in a World War II concentration camp with her radiant testimony of the power of God intact. Then years later, she was speaking at a church service in Munich when:

> I saw him, the former S.S. man who had stood guard at the shower room door in the processing center at Ravensbruck. He was the first of our actual jailers that I had seen since that time. And suddenly it was all there—the roomful of mocking men, the heaps of clothing, Betsie's pain-blanched face.

He came up to me as the church was emptying, beaming and bowing. "How grateful I am for your message, Fraulein," he said. "To think that, as you say, He has washed my sins away!"

His hand was thrust out to shake mine. And I, who had preached so often . . . the need to forgive, kept my hand at my side.

Even as the angry, vengeful thoughts boiled through me, I saw the sin of them. Jesus Christ had died for this man; was I going to ask for more? Lord Jesus, I prayed, forgive me and help me to forgive him.

I tried to smile, I struggled to raise my hand. I could not. I felt nothing, not the slightest spark of warmth or charity. And so again I breathed a silent prayer. Jesus, I cannot forgive him. Give me your forgiveness.

As I took his hand the most incredible thing happened. From my shoulder along my arm and through my hand a current seemed to pass from me to him, while into my heart sprang a love for this stranger that almost overwhelmed me.

And so I discovered that it is not on our forgiveness any more than on our goodness that the world's healing hinges, but on His. When He tells us to love our enemies, He gives, along with the command, the love itself. (*The Hiding Place*, p. 239.)

Not all of us will have such great wrongs to forgive, but all of us must learn how to forgive the wrongs that *are* inflicted on us. Let's remember Corrie's lesson—that our Savior will give us the means of fulfilling this commandment if we struggle to do our part. I gained another insight when I read the account of Sister Eileen Starr. Her mother dutifully cooked meals for her and her sister and bought their clothes, but the children "felt deprived—emotionally deprived—by our mother. As adults, we have endlessly discussed the lack of warmth, approval, constructive criticism, moral training, and hospitality that existed in our home. Why was Mother . . . uncaring, critical, and self-centered?"

Eileen joined the Church, where she was mothered by other women, but the hurt lingered. When she went to the temple to be baptized on behalf of her deceased mother, she wept all the way there from her sorrow and hurt. But, she writes, "When I rose up out of the water, a healing balm . . . washed away all of my bitterness and longing. I saw Mother, stalwart and whole. The Holy Ghost filled me with the awareness that my mother had been handicapped in mortal life. She had had an emotional handicap, the source of which remains a secret to me. But she is handicapped no longer. And neither am I." ("Forgiving My Mother," *Ensign*, August 1990, p. 49.)

There are parts of our mortal experience that we simply will not be able to understand in this life. In those cases, we must be willing to forgive on faith. Sister Starr's willingness to forgive her mother and perform this saving ordinance for her, even though her mother had hurt her deeply through her emotional coldness, opened a door of understanding. Now, she says, "How thankful I am for the Savior and for his love, which extends to me and to my now-whole mother, who is learning the lessons she could not learn in mortal life. I am eager to meet her and to share the love with her we both were deprived of on earth."

So, if courage is the first demand of our day, forgiveness is the second.

The third characteristic we need for the day in which we live is the ability to minister. Belle Spafford, the ninth general president of the Relief Society, always proofread her own letters. On one occasion, she noted that she had meant to write to a stake Relief Society president, "It's always such a joy to hear from you." But there was a typographical error. Instead of typing J-O-Y, her secretary had typed J-O-B. Her happy greeting had come out, "It's always such a job to hear from you."

In this inadvertent slip, Sister Spafford captured the dilemma we often face. Often we have callings that we want to be a joy to us and to each other, but they turn into a job. We get trapped in meetings, lists, assignments, projects, arrangements, negotiations, and planning. In other words, we turn into administrators. And the joy of our callings gets squeezed out under the weight of these jobs. Joy comes from serving others and delighting in our sisterhood—in ministering to rather than administering for each other.

Isn't it terrible to think that we might be neglecting the spiritual gifts of faith, hope, and charity in favor of checklists and assignments? Or to realize that we might be spending more time on refreshments and centerpieces than on the gifts of discernment, testimony, and prophecy by which we could truly minister to our sisters? In our general Relief Society presidency, Elaine and Aileen and I don't spend very much time looking at statistics that come in. We certainly don't compare wards and stakes. Instead, we pray that personal testimonies and charity will increase, that individual women and their families will be blessed by the Relief Society, and that we will enjoy a unified sisterhood.

You, in whatever callings you have throughout your own life, will face many choices between serving the program and serving an individual. I believe that if we truly serve individuals in the Lord's way, we'll have less trouble with the program. There's a wonderful story about President McKay that illustrates the distinction. Irene Bates tells the story, which involved her husband, Bill, the first British president of Manchester Stake in England during the 1960s.

It was customary for the stake presidents and two bishops, chosen in turn, to be invited to attend general conference, with traveling expenses being paid by the Church. In this particular year, the instructions came to bring all of the bishops and branch presidents.

"Bill was sure this was an error," recalls Sister Bates, "and so he waited for the correction to come." It didn't, so he called N. Eldon Tanner, then president of the European Mission. President Tanner confirmed that the instructions indeed said to invite bishops and branch presidents — "all of them." Still Bill hesitated. Finally, President Tanner called him: "I'm waiting for the names from your stake," he reminded Bill.

Bill, still with secret trepidation, obediently issued the invitations. The bishops and branch presidents were delighted with the prospect of coming to Salt Lake City, a once-in-a-lifetime opportunity for most of them. Then, the very next Monday, Bill received word that the first instructions had in fact been in error. He was told to select two bishops and tell the rest that they would not be able to go.

Bill was heartsick, especially for Brother Vernon, the branch president in the small town of Rawtenstall. The Church was his whole life. He and his wife willingly opened their small home for the branch meetings, and Brother Vernon used to moonlight by digging ditches to earn money for the building fund. People in that tiny branch used to pay tithing and then walk to work so they could make ends meet. Bill knew that the forthcoming trip had been a major celebration, not only in the branch but in the town as well. With great pride, the local paper had featured the forthcoming trip. Brother Vernon's employer had been gracious and eager to give him time off work. Everyone was simply thrilled. It was the innocence of that anticipation that Bill could not bear to think of disappointing.

Bill lay awake all night, trying to think of a plan. He was willing to give Brother Vernon his own place, but that would have revealed the situation. We would willingly have paid his expenses ourselves; but if he were not officially invited, he wouldn't have a place reserved at the meetings. Finally, in deep distress, he phoned . . . Marion D. Hanks, president of the British Mission, explained the situation, and said, "I don't see anything to do but to call President McKay and lay the situation before him." President Hanks replied warmly, "I couldn't advise you to do that, President Bates, but here's President McKay's direct number."

Bill hung up the phone and looked at the number for a long moment, then said, "I've got to do it." He went back in the office while I waited outside. He got straight through to President McKay's secretary, who put him straight through to President McKay. Bill poured out the whole story while President McKay listened without saying a word. At the end, while Bill waited in an agony of suspense, President McKay said, "I see," and paused thoughtfully. After the longest ten seconds in Bill's life, President McKay said, "You're quite right, President Bates. It would be very wrong to do that to that good man. We must have them all come. Please do me a favor and let *me* call President Tanner."

Bill came out of the office with tears streaming down his face. Within a day, he had word from President Tanner that the original instructions were to stand. Brother Vernon and the others went. They had a wonderful experience, particularly Brother Vernon. He came back infused with new life, feeling connected to the Church as he never had before. Proudly the local newspaper reported his experience and views. The whole tiny branch basked in reflected glory. And they never knew. (As quoted in David Lawrence McKay, *My Father, David O. McKay* [Salt Lake City: Deseret Book, 1989], pp. 258–59.)

Doesn't that decision seem right! I imagine that somewhere, in some office, somebody shook his head and said, "That President McKay! Always changing the instructions. Why can't he just follow the program?" But I really think that Jesus would have been as delighted as President Bates at the compassion shown.

We face the challenges of our day, as Esther faced the challenges of hers. But we do not face them alone. Our Father will give us the courage to stand for what is right, the gift of forgiveness when the inevitable wrongs occur, and the steadfast willingness to minister gladly and sensitively to others, one at a time, as the Savior ministers to us.

CHAPTER SIX

# "A House of Glory"

MOST OF US THINK OF THE TEMPLE when we hear the description recorded in the Doctrine and Covenants of "a house of prayer, a house of fasting, a house of faith, a house of learning, a house of glory, a house of order, a house of God." (D&C 88:119.) And justifiably so. But this scripture was given six months before the ground was broken for the building of the Kirtland Temple. At the time, the Saints didn't know what a temple was, or what it was for, or what they would do in it. And when the Kirtland Temple was finished, it was not a place that could be entered only by recommend. It was a public place, a place where the Saints came together with their children, their friends—even their enemies, I imagine—to worship and learn together. In other words, it was something like a meetinghouse when it was built.

There's a parallel here for our day. A "house of glory . . . a house of God" can be our own ward meetinghouse, even our own Relief Society room. Or, consider yet another concept about temples, discussed in Paul's letter to the Corinthians: "Know ye not that *ye* are the temple of God, and that the Spirit of God dwelleth in *you*?" (1 Corinthians 3:16; emphasis added.)

I love the way Paul says that: "Know ye not?" It's as though he is astonished that he must remind his readers about the indwelling Spirit of God, something so obvious that they should know it already. Is it possible that when we talk about "a house of glory . . . a house of God," we are talking about ourselves? Another thing I love about that scripture is that the Spirit is already there, even though the Corinthians have forgotten about it. Paul doesn't say, "If you're very good and work like galley slaves and do every single thing on this three-page list of *How to Be a Good Christian*, it's possible that *maybe* the Spirit of God will visit you for a minute or two." No, he says the Spirit of God is already in us, even though we may not feel it or may not recognize it or may not be doing everything we should. That's a thought to give us courage.

I like to think about the "house of glory" in three ways. The first way, of course, is our temples, which are dedicated as "the house of the Lord." The second way is to think of the temple as the Kirtland Temple—as a meetinghouse or chapel where we can come together without any entrance requirements and strengthen and learn from each other. And the third way is to know and feel deep within ourselves that I—and you, and each person in the world—is a temple of God and that we are holy. All three concepts help us with the important task of strengthening ourselves spiritually to face the challenges of today.

How would you like to feel strong, even invincible? Paul says, "I can do all things through Christ which strengtheneth me." (Philippians 4:13.) That's a glorious promise. Have you had moments in your life when you've felt this way? And have there been moments when you've felt just the opposite—afraid, angry, unworthy, unloved, unlovable? Those feelings do not come from God. They *don't!* What God wants for you is feelings of glory. And what he wants to give you is gloriousness, here and hereafter. His spirit is dwelling in you right now. And it doesn't leave, even if you feel too despairing or too frightened and too inadequate to feel it anymore. It's there.

There are three concepts that help me understand how Paul's secret works. The first is that God wants you—not somebody else, not you in ten years, not a perfect you, but you right now. Consider this experience of Sharon Lee Swenson, a faculty member at Brigham Young University, when she was called as Relief Society president in her ward in Salt Lake City:

"All my life, I have felt that someday I would be great and valuable. Someday. Not now, not yet. But someday, I'd do everything just right. I'd be slim, attractive, and soft-spoken, without a semi-lisp and southern Utah drawl. When I opened my dresser drawers, I would see neatly folded clothes with crocheted sachets nestled among them. I would have a spotless refrigerator filled with healthy, delicious food. I'd read poetry and would have abandoned my current need for regulator doses of strong murder mysteries. But I knew I wasn't that person then.

"The witness I received . . . was that the Lord wanted me—murder mysteries, mixed-up drawers, and all, complete with failings and weaknesses. I was loved of the Lord and had something important to give my sisters. That something was I, myself." ("The Amazement of Grace," *Dialogue*, Winter 1988, p. 98.)

That's all the Lord wants of you—you, yourself. And that's all you can give. You can't be someone you aren't. You can't give someone else's gift. Who and what you are is enough, and each gift, given like this, is glorious! The Doctrine and Covenants explains, "The Lord requireth the heart and a willing mind." (D&C 64:34.) It doesn't say that the Lord requires competence, or a Ph.D., or immaculate housekeeping, or professional success. But it doesn't say that he'll be satisfied with a half-hearted you, either. He wants your whole heart, and for good reason. Real power does not lie in external forces, but in the heart. Gary Zukow, a modern philosopher, says:

"An evil person can be arrested, but can evil be arrested? An evil group can be imprisoned, but can evil be imprisoned? A compassionate heart is more effective against evil than an army. An army can engage another army, but it cannot engage evil. A compassionate heart can engage evil directly—it can bring Light where there was no Light.

"Understanding evil [as darkness—or the absence of light] . . . requires you to examine the choices that you make each moment in terms of whether they move you toward Light or away from it. It allows you to look with compassion upon those who engage in evil activities, even as you challenge those activities. . . . It permits you to see that the place to begin the task of eliminating evil is within yourself. This is the appropriate response to evil." (*The Seat of the Soul* [New York: Simon and Schuster, 1990], p. 72.)

The second secret is that the world and the Church will give you many messages about what you should be doing, and many different opportunities and invitations to contribute, but *you* get to choose.

On one occasion I was assigned to visit teach a sister who had a large family of young children, virtually no income, and poor health. It was obvious to me after one visit that she really needed someone who could sometimes take care of her children while she went to the doctor or did her grocery shopping. And my circumstances were such that I couldn't be that person right then. I explained the situation to the Relief Society president and asked for a change in assignment so that need could be met. On the other hand, I was a terrific visiting teacher for a lonely woman whose needs I could help meet by making a ten-minute phone call from work two or three times a week.

The third secret is that the Lord has no universal time clocks or schedules; only individual ones. The scriptures have never commanded us to do everything right the first time or to get it all done by Tuesday. On the contrary, they say, "Do not run faster or labor more than you have strength and means," and speak of "rejoic[ing] as a strong man to run a race." (D&C 10:4; Psalm 19:5.) Isn't that a wonderful image—of someone rising to a challenge with strength that rejoices in that exact challenge? There is a marvelous poem by Emma Lou Thayne that talks about how to avoid feelings pressured by time:

*About Time*

*Each of us wants to be friends with time,*
*Comfortable waiting for toast to pop,*

*Pleased to pull at the garden knowing*
*no season is going off without us.*

*The trick is to find out*
*whether a minute is worth more*

*crammed or empty.*
*And, either way, to get on with it.*

(*As for Me and My House: Meditations on Living and Loving* [Salt Lake City: Bookcraft, 1989], p. 17. Used by permission.)

No one else can make the decision for you about that minute. It's up to you.

Right now, my timetable includes Relief Society, a whole lot of Relief Society, and not much else besides Relief Society. No one ever tells us, when we're called, how long it will be for; but a lot of things will just have to wait until after these Relief Society years are over. My patriarchal blessing promises me that "many records" of my kin "shall be made available" to me, and that I will rejoice in the success of my labors. So that's somewhere on the timetable, but how foolish I would be to fret because I think I have to do it now!

We need to be patient with ourselves if things don't seem to be happening for us the way we think they should. I can't think about the temple as a "house of glory" without remembering my first temple experience. By the time Ed and I were able to be sealed, we were living in Salt Lake City. I remember how impressed I was with the beauty of the temple and also with the instruction. I liked moving from room to room, ascending higher as we learned each new stage. But I was also uncomfortable. It was strange. I didn't know what to do. I felt awkward. I was so grateful for Jennie and Thomas Beisinger, the missionaries who helped Ed and me through that first time, and for the other sisters who helped me on return visits when I was sneaking sideways peeks trying to figure out what to do next. But I was patient with myself and my feelings, and now I'm very comfortable with the temple. I walk in as though I were walking into my own home, with the same sense of being welcome and at home.

I've often heard wonderful stories of people who have seen visions in the temple or had experiences with the individual for whom they were officiating, and I've thought, "Okay, today I have Maria So-and-So's name. I wonder if she's here. I wonder if I'll feel her presence." But I never have. Does that mean I'm not as spiritual as the people who have those manifestations? Or that I should stop going to the temple? Not at all. I *do* have spiritual experiences. Don't think your spiritual experiences have to look the same as those you read about in the *Ensign* or hear about in testimony meeting.

The temple is a wonderful place of instruction, but I've never found it to be a place where I had much time for meditating on any particular problem I've needed to solve. Instead, I've appreciated the chance to receive instruction and perform a service for someone else, then I've taken that instruction away and pondered it in my own heart and in my own home, exploring ways to apply it to my problems. Furthermore, not everyone has access to the temple, but we all have access to the spirit of the temple, because it's the same spirit of the Lord that dwells within us.

We don't have to be in a sacred place for spiritual things to happen. The Sacred Grove was just a stand of trees before Joseph Smith walked into it. It became sacred because of what happened there. Where is your Sacred Grove? It could even be in your car, if that's where you spend a lot of time thinking through problems and attuning your heart sensitively to the Spirit. Perhaps it's while you're out walking. Heavenly Father doesn't save up all his spiritual experiences just for sacrament meeting or the temple.

And that's because *you're* a temple—a living, breathing, walking temple on two legs with a spirit that's in motion, seeing the needs of many, meeting the needs of many, sometimes tuned in fully and beautifully to the indwelling Spirit of the Lord, and sometimes even forgetting that that Spirit is there, and needing Paul's reminder.

I love the story of Elijah seeking the Lord on Mount Horeb at a time when he felt he had nothing left to live for. The children of Israel had forsaken the Lord for idols and had slain the prophets. "And I, even I only, am left," he said. Have you ever felt like that, so abandoned and all alone? The Lord told Elijah to stand out on the mount: "And, behold, the Lord passed by, and a great and strong wind rent the mountains, and brake in pieces the rocks before the Lord; but the Lord was not in the wind; and after the wind an earthquake; but the Lord was not in the earthquake: and after the earthquake a fire; but the Lord was not in the fire: and after the fire a still small voice." (1 Kings 19:10–12.)

Elijah, who had stood unmoved looking on the earthquake, the terrible wind, and the fire, heard that still small voice and wrapped his face in his mantle.

We need to listen to that still small voice rather than to the thunderous crashes of public opinion, or the fiery words of people who want us to follow their solutions, or the earth-shaking fears and disapprovals of our associates.

Learn to hear what the Spirit tells you. The Lord knows you in ways other people couldn't possibly.

I love the Lord with all my heart. Words are inadequate to capture and express that love. That's why I thrill so to the scriptures where those human writers stretched themselves and the limits of their language to try to express their own love. I know exactly how Ammon was feeling when he said: "I do not boast in my own strength, nor in my own wisdom; but behold, my joy is full, yea, my heart is brim with joy, and I will rejoice in my God. Yea, I know that I am nothing; as to my strength I am weak; therefore I will not boast of myself, but I will boast of my God, for in his strength I can do all things. . . . Behold, who can glory too much in the Lord? Yea, who can say too much of his great power, and of his mercy, and of his long-suffering towards [us]? Behold, I say unto you, I cannot say the smallest part which I feel." (Alma 26:11–12, 16.)

Consider something Paul said: "Rejoice in the Lord always. I will say it again: Rejoice! Let your gentleness be evident to all. The Lord is near. Do not be anxious about anything, but in everything, by prayer and petition, *with thanksgiving*, present your requests to God. And the peace of God, which transcends all understanding, will guard your hearts and your minds in Christ Jesus." (NIV, Philippians 4:4–7; italics added.)

Have you felt that peace and thanksgiving? When you *are* feeling it, do you have to force yourself to be pleasant to your family? Do you feel reluctant to serve someone else? Do you yawn when you pick up the scriptures? Do you hurry through your prayers?

I know we don't feel this way all the time. There's never a whole day of complete happiness in anyone's life, but these moments are given to us as moments. We need to accept such moments and rejoice in them and let them sustain us when the next moment isn't quite so glorious.

We live in challenging times. They are wonderful days; but they are also troubled days, days of wickedness and vengeance, days when Satan shadows the earth with the great chain of his bondage and laughs as he shakes that chain. (See Moses 7:26.) But we are the holy temples of the Lord. We are, each one of us, a house of glory, a house of God. Dwelling within each of us is the Spirit of the Lord, even when we don't feel as though that Spirit is there, even when we need to be reminded — "Know ye not?"

"For God, who commanded the light to shine out of darkness, hath shined in our hearts, to give the light of the knowledge of the glory of God in the face of Jesus Christ." (2 Corinthians 4:6.)

# CHAPTER SEVEN

# Motherhood: Less Guilt, More Joy

IN SOME WAYS, I AM AN UNLIKELY person to share thoughts on motherhood. Many people have an image of Mormon mothers that includes a large number of children, an intensely concerned style of mothering, and motherhood as a full-time occupation, complete with fresh bread, hot cookies, and cold milk waiting for the children as they come scrambling in the door from school.

I don't fit many of those images. I am the mother of two and have worked most of my adult life as an educator. And when it came to scrambling, everyone in our family did it.

That eight-children-and-cookies "image" of Mormon motherhood is a stereotype, of course; I certainly have no intention of replacing it with another one of, say, two children and a briefcase. But there's another element that goes along with the eight children that often is not a stereotype, but a reality. And that's guilt.

During my time as a member of the Relief Society general presidency, I have received a startling education about the amount of inappropriate guilt that literally hundreds of wonderful Latter-day Saint women feel about the subject of motherhood. I have been astonished to learn that many never-married women feel guilty and unworthy because they are not mothers. Many married women who have fertility problems feel guilty that they cannot bear children. Mothers feel guilty that they have too many children, or too few. Many others worry because they are not perfect mothers or because they don't have perfect children. When their children make mistakes or life choices that seem wrong, these mothers are racked by suffering—not only for the painful consequences their beloved children must experience, but by the even more painful suffering of personal guilt that springs from their feeling they have somehow failed.

I am probably exaggerating. I know many happy mothers who find great joy in their children. But it does seem that I have encountered an excessive amount of heartbreak clustered around motherhood. It has opened my eyes to a whole new dimension of many women's experiences.

I respect this suffering and pain. But I think it is often misplaced. If some of these wonderful women are feeling burdened and grieved by their motherhood instead of rejoicing in it, perhaps it is because they have picked up burdens that are not necessary for them to carry.

Perhaps we can explore three ideas together that will help us put down such unnecessary burdens. We must (1) accept struggle and imperfection as facts of life, not as judgments or punishment, (2) accept many partners in parenting, and (3) respect the agency of our children.

ACCEPT IMPERFECTION AS A FACT

I strongly feel that we should expect struggles and imperfections in this life. The most realistic expectation we can make of ourselves is to do our best. We should not expect to control outcomes, either for ourselves or for our children.

I grew up expecting that circumstances would probably never be ideal, but knowing that my task was to struggle to do my best in those less-than-ideal circumstances. I learned this lesson early from my mother, Hatsuko Nishi Nishimura.

One of my earliest memories is sitting on the floor next to my mother, with both of us reflected in a large mirror. I had misbehaved in some way, and I was expecting a scolding; instead, mother told me about her own childhood. Left motherless at the age of eleven, she had raised her two younger sisters, teaching herself how to make their clothes, carefully eking out her father's meager wages, hiding at lunchtime so the other children wouldn't notice that she had nothing to eat but a rice ball, and eventually having to give up school altogether in the sixth grade. I remember looking at both of us, reflected in the mirror. I sensed on some level, child though I was, that my mother's strength and determination could be reflected in me. I saw her serenity, love, and wisdom; I knew that life had not defeated her, and that I could make the same choices. That mother-daughter image has sustained me many times when I have wondered if I had the strength to continue a course or to achieve a goal.

In my case, much of what I would call my severest struggle came in my desire to gain an education. Mother was a bright woman, constantly learning new things. Even as a child I knew that, so I must have sensed her pain at having to leave school and her determination that I must get an education.

I have three younger brothers; but for five years, I was my parents' only child. Perhaps it was for this reason, perhaps it was because they were in a new country, perhaps it was because my parents lived under the strict domination of my paternal grandparents for the first ten or twelve years of their marriage that they dreamed different dreams for me. The mother-in-law/daughter-in-law relationship in Japan can be especially harsh, and I know that my mother struggled with serving and pleasing her mother-in-law, even though she never complained. I think it must also have been a struggle for my father, the oldest son, to give his hard-earned money to his father, then to receive back what my grandfather thought was adequate to feed and clothe the family.

My parents, from the time I was tiny, impressed the importance of an education on me. They always expressed acceptance of their own lives but said, "For you, you must seek something better. You must get an education." I never remember my mother telling me to work for a specific goal, but she taught me three principles: Work hard. Do your very best. And be happy in what you do.

I had a chance to test the strength of these principles at a young age. When I was fifteen and World War II broke out, severe gas rationing was imposed. Our little village was twelve miles away from the town of Hawi where the middle school was, and gas was available only for the elementary school buses. We faced a dilemma. Should I stop going to school and hope the war would end soon? Should I move to the town and keep going to school? If I did that, what would we do for money? My parents and I talked it over. Somehow, there was only one real choice: I must get my education.

I moved to the town and became a maid for a couple who taught orchestra and English at school. It was hard. At the age of fifteen, I was in charge of the food budget. I would get up at 5:00, cook breakfast, clean house, make the beds, and go off to school at 8:30. When I came home, I would shop, clean, and cook dinner, then study in the evening until eleven or twelve o'clock.

Some nights I would lie in bed feeling overwhelmed and afraid of the magnitude of my challenges. But I was sustained by two things: I knew the life I was leading there did not stretch endlessly before me but was preparing me for a better future. And I knew that having to struggle was not wrong. Struggle was part of life. This was part of the legacy mother had given me.

One of the stories my mother told me was about a boy named Ninomia Kinjiro who was devoted simultaneously to two Japanese ideals: serving his family and revering education. He loved school but left to help his mother when she needed to support the family. He helped by gathering firewood in the forest. Yet he did not relinquish his desire for an education. He would walk home from the forest carrying an enormous bundle of twigs and sticks lashed to his back and an open book in his hands. Years later, when my husband was president of the Osaka Japan Mission, I saw a statue of Ninomia Kinjiro with his bundle of sticks and his book in a little town near Osaka. It was like meeting an old friend.

## ACCEPT MANY PARTNERS IN PARENTING

Mother taught me that I was strong enough to sustain the struggle of life, that I could achieve despite less-than-perfect circumstances. That in itself was an extraordinary gift, but so was the fact that she released me to that struggle, without trying to protect me from it. She had to have confidence that I could meet many of my own physical and emotional needs and that, in areas where I could not, others would supply the parenting I needed.

As a mother now, I can't imagine how difficult that must have been for her. But during my three years in high school, the foundation of my mother's teachings gave me the courage to try. As I learned by doing, I taught myself many new things and developed the confidence that I could do almost anything if I were willing to work long and hard enough.

I missed my mother and father. I was lonesome for my little brothers. When gasoline became more available after 1942, my father would save his gas coupons and come for me on Sunday afternoons. I would get home from church and see my mother and little brothers sitting in the car, craning their necks for the first sight of me. How my heart would leap with joy, and how I would race to be with them! We would go home for the afternoon and evening, and then my father would bring me back early Monday morning for another long week. I knew that he would walk nearly everywhere he went, saving the precious, rationed gasoline so that, in a week or two, I could come home again.

When my own sons went away to school and on their missions, I realized how steadfastly a mother's heart can yearn for an absent child, even though she wants him to be where he is and has faith that he is doing a good thing. My mother must have yearned for me in the same way. But by entrusting me to myself and to others, she gave me strength to reach my goal.

Her confidence was not misplaced. I found unexpected reserves of strength in myself. My employer's confidence that I could budget correctly and make my way through exotic recipes gave me confidence to try. All of my teachers were extremely supportive, but my speech and business teachers made a special point of talking with me, encouraging me, finding out how things were going, and giving me any help I needed. Once, when I needed a gown for the junior prom, my former sixth-grade teacher sewed me a lovely dress — I still wore it in college. The missionaries and members of Halaula Branch were unfailingly supportive in the best possible way. They taught me how to fast, pray, exercise faith, and seek answers in the scriptures. In so doing, they gave me tools that have served me all my life.

It is unusual in this culture and this time period for children to leave home in their early teens, but all children reach the point at which they need to leave home. Parents need to prepare themselves to send their children on their way rejoicing. Most parents I know conscientiously teach children how to care for themselves, make a home, get along with others, work independently, and prepare themselves to earn a living. Sometimes mismatched timetables can create a problem. A child may be both psychologically and physically prepared to leave home, but the parents are not yet ready. It is a recipe for conflict.

When my husband was called to preside over the Japan Okinawa Mission in 1968, we had a wonderful three-year experience in parenthood. When President Spencer W. Kimball interviewed us, he asked Ed, "What do you think your number-one job is?"

Ed replied, "To work with the members, to keep them strong, and to baptize others as members."

"Your number-one job," President Kimball responded, "is with the missionaries. You have the responsibility for two hundred children. See that their testimonies increase and that they complete an honorable mission."

We set the goal of not sending a single missionary home early. We succeeded, but it was difficult. When elders telephoned and said, "I can't take any more. I'm going home," we would say, "Let's talk about it. Come in to the mission home." Ed would talk to them and I would mother them. They would find their faltering faith growing stronger, and soon they would be out in the field again. I really felt like a mother. I knew where every one of our two hundred missionaries was assigned and could stamp the mail for forwarding in ten minutes while the commissarian would need to look up locations and addresses. As each missionary came in, I cooked him or her a sukiyaki dinner, and Ed and I sent back a photograph to the parents with a letter telling what we appreciated about that missionary.

Ed was strict about the missionaries keeping the rules. They were supposed to be up at 5:30 A.M., so he often knocked on their apartment doors promptly at that hour. After an interview, he would buy eggs and sausage and cook breakfast for them. I always sent a sheet cake for the elders in the district, so even if they had a rebuke coming, they felt an increase of love from us. Once when Ed was interviewing an elder, I organized the other three elders in the apartment, and we gave it the cleaning of its life. After we finished, one elder looked around and sighed, "Oh, Sister Okazaki, we just needed a mom."

I tried to do other things their mothers would do. Some young men thought that a well-balanced meal meant a hamburger in each hand. I taught them how to make lasagna by substituting tofu for cottage cheese. When one Arizona elder was terribly homesick for tacos and begged me (of all people) for a tortilla recipe, I found one, practiced until I could make it, and sent out instructions in the monthly letter. It worked! I nearly always accompanied Ed when he conducted the bimonthly missionary interviews. Sometimes these were severe sessions in which he would lay down the law, reprimanding and challenging. When the missionary came out looking chastened, I would encourage and console.

We felt grateful to parents for sending us their children and tried to behave as we thought they would in those circumstances. Many parents expressed their gratitude to us for being important to their sons and daughters during those crucial mission years.

All of us must be willing to accept many partners in our parenting. Too often we feel that we can do it all or that we should do it all. As a schoolteacher and later as a principal, I encountered many wonderfully concerned and supportive parents. They were eager to help their children learn and became true partners in that process. They respected my perspective as a teacher and my expertise as a trained professional. I respected their knowledge of their children and their ability to foster learning at home. But other parents insisted on "mothering" long-distance. I was never quite sure if they wanted me to be their child's second mother or if they wanted to be their own child's teacher. If Jason had a problem in grasping the concept of addition, they had a long list of activities, approaches, drills, and solutions to that problem. If Jason had a social problem, they were equally quick with a list of solutions they wanted me to apply. They were anxious, tense, and intense. I respected their concern, but I saw children who were anxious, fretful, and stressed as a result.

I have thought often about the mother of Moses. What a wonderful example of a mother who did the best she could under difficult circumstances! What if she had insisted on being an "intensive" mother, refusing to let Moses out of her arms, hovering over him constantly, counting every breath he drew? He would have been subject to the fate Pharaoh decreed for the other Israelite babies: "Every son that is born ye shall cast into the river." (Exodus 1:22.) Instead, she let him go by literally "casting" him into the river—but prepared to float. She let another woman mother her son all the years he was growing up; and because she did, Moses was later in a position to save not only his family but his entire nation. How grateful the entire house of Israel could be that Moses' mother did not insist on being Moses' only mother.

Each family and each couple must make the best decision they can for their own children. For Ed and me, a very even-handed partnership in parenting worked best of all. Ed helped to bathe, dress, and feed our boys from the time they were infants. He loved playing with them. I nearly always did the cooking, but Ed nearly always did the dishes. During the week, we took turns being with the children while the other one did whatever else needed to be done—cleaning, laundry, and shopping. On the weekends, we could be together full time as a family—playing and going on outings, working on projects together, and worshiping together. When Ken or Bob became ill, Ed and I took turns missing work to stay home with the sick child. When there were programs or sports events that the boys participated in, we also took turns. I do not recall those years as stressful. We just did our best and didn't worry about the rest.

We didn't fuss about finding care for the children when we needed it — sitters, nursery school, and preschool. We were very careful to get the best caregivers, the best teachers, the best situations we could — then we counted on these people to do their best with our boys. We didn't think we could do it all ourselves, we didn't try to do it all ourselves, and we didn't worry because we couldn't do it all ourselves.

We appreciated the skills and dedication of the caregivers, Primary teachers, schoolteachers, Scoutmasters, and parents of friends, all of whom shared themselves with our sons and taught them in their own ways. Parley Love and his wife ran a nursery school that was truly a place of love. Our boys never fussed about going there but, on the contrary, were excited and happy to go to "Parley's place." Parley did much more than administer the program. He knew our boys as individuals, spent time with them, praised and encouraged them, and gave them a unique experience.

It seemed wonderfully reciprocal to me that I was in a position as an educator to share parenting back. I knew I had a great deal to give the children in my classroom, and I felt a responsibility that extended to children beyond my own. I feel so rewarded when someone comes up to me and says, "You don't remember me, but . . . " and I see one of "my children" looking eagerly out of an adult face. One mother used to tell me, "Doug is so well organized, and I know where he got it. The other three don't have anywhere near that ability." Then she would add with a laugh, "I can say exactly the same thing at home, but when *you* say it, they take it seriously." For every child, there is something important about having someone outside the family explain a value held in the family. All parents need partners. And what I did for someone else's child, someone else was doing for mine.

## RESPECT YOUR CHILDREN'S AGENCY

Perhaps because I was a teacher, I knew that children had their own individuality. Whenever I saw a parent trying too hard to make one child fit the family mold, I flinched a little. I knew there would be trouble.

As the gospel plan makes so beautifully plain, our agency is eternal. It seems to have existed even before we took the form of spirit children. Apparently our Heavenly Father, by nature, will not violate our agency. Why, then, should we be surprised to find that our own children have wills? Each spirit is unique. It follows, then, that trying to make people think, feel, or even behave in the same way—except for those ways which are necessary for an orderly society—is an attempt to counter the way the universe works. How could anyone expect to succeed?

As Ed and I raised our sons, we tried to find ways to let them explore and express their individuality. When Ken decided he wanted to play the accordion, we saw that he had lessons. We hoped Bob would want to play the piano and even bought one—but no, it was the accordion for him, too. When Ken expressed an interest in art, we took in summer sessions at the Art Barn. When the boys decided they wanted to ski, Ed faithfully drove them to the slopes every Saturday. (It wasn't long until they lured first him, then me too, into skiing.)

A tougher challenge came in Japan when the boys, then teenagers, decided they wanted to wear their hair long. We had always prized their independence of mind and allowed them to make as many of their own decisions as possible, but this one was hard. The Saints in Japan had strict ideas about how a mission president's sons should look, and we were concerned about the association of the long hair with drugs—which we knew were available at the boys' school. We talked it over with them, with each other, and with the Lord. And finally it seemed clear to us: it was far more important to us that they pay their tithing, attend their meetings, and administer the sacrament worthily than it was for their hair to be a certain length. We were not going to fight over something that was, in the last analysis, not very important. So they went to school with long hair and accompanied us home from the mission field with long hair. When members commented about their hair, Ed had a kind way of saying, "They have their agency," that ended the discussion.

Ed and I were not perfect parents. I know that we made many mistakes. Nor do we have perfect children. But we never expected to! We expected to work hard, to struggle with imperfect circumstances, to find all the moments of happiness and joy that we could along the way, and to accept the less-than-perfect results with thanksgiving. As I read the scriptural narratives that involve families, I do not see perfection. I see mothers and fathers struggling with imperfect situations, all of them trying to do their best for their children. And I see children who made different choices from each other, choices that brought joy to their parents, choices that brought them sorrow. Adam and Eve taught all of their children the gospel. Some accepted it, some didn't. One of the most beautiful scriptures of their married life together shows us how they managed to put things in perspective. When Adam understood the gospel plan, he cried, "Blessed be the name of God, for because of my transgression my eyes are opened, and in this life I shall have joy, and again in the flesh I shall see God. And Eve, his wife, heard all these things and was glad, saying: Were it not for our transgression we never should have had seed, and never should have known good and evil, and the joy of our redemption, and the eternal life which God giveth unto all the obedient." (Moses 5:10–11.)

Cain was surely a beloved son, surely a son who was taught the gospel. Yet he made a series of choices that brought him to that awful moment when he stood over his murdered brother's body. It is significant to me that the story in Genesis leaves Adam's and Eve's activities to follow Cain for some time, recounting his confrontation with the Lord, his punishment, and his life in exile as he founds his own city and family (See Genesis 4:1–24.) Virtually the whole chapter is given over to this recital. Only in the last two verses do we come back to Adam and Eve. Does the scripture tell us how they grieved over Abel's murder? No, although surely they did. Does it tell us about the confusion, anger, and sorrow they might have felt over Cain's rash deed and exile? No, although they possibly felt these things. Does the author of Genesis scold Adam and Eve for not teaching Cain properly? No, there is no suggestion of rebuke. Instead, Adam and Eve, comforting each other in their sorrow, conceive a son whom Eve names Seth, "for God, said she, hath appointed me another seed instead of Abel, whom Cain slew." (Genesis 4:25.) In other words, life literally went on for Adam and Eve!

Most parents cannot give birth to another child when they lose a child to disobedience or rebellion. But they can make the same decision metaphorically that Adam and Eve did—to acknowledge their terrible loss and decide that life goes on regardless. There are times when our best is not good enough to save another. We can acknowledge our loss and grieve over it, but surely we must also learn from it that life goes on. Besides, I would be slow to say that any child is irretrievably lost. Sometimes a child needs to be an adult and even a parent for many years before he or she has the strength and wisdom to rebuild a parent-child relationship that was damaged years before.

It was obvious that Ed and I were doing things differently from most of the traditional families in our various wards, but I honestly cannot ever recall feeling disapproval from anyone. I wonder if we would feel differently if our boys had turned out differently. We expected them to grow up to be compassionate and committed members of the Church, to think for themselves and make reasonable decisions, and to be competent at their chosen work. They are. One son is married and has two children; we expect him and his wife to make responsible decisions together about their life-style and about caring for their boys. And they do. We love all four of them and think they're wonderful.

Our other son is unmarried. I was astounded to hear one mother fret about a son over twenty-five who had not married, wondering what she had done wrong in raising him. My son's marital status is his business, not mine. He is a responsible individual who is contributing to society. He is a clear thinker and a loving human being. Other people tell us about his generosity with his time and money, or we find out about his "special projects" by accident. If and when he marries, I'll enjoy his wife as I enjoy my other son's wife. For now, I enjoy him as a single person. And one of the things I like most about him is that he instantly identifies and summarily rejects attempts to make him feel guilty about not being married. How foolish I would be to pick up the guilt my son has properly rejected and bind it on my own shoulders, to create a burden where none exists!

The scriptures tell us of a religious ritual of the ancient Hebrews. On the Day of Atonement, the high priest would bring two goats before the congregation at the tabernacle. Lots would be cast. One goat would be sacrificed for a sin offering, but the other "shall be presented alive before the Lord, to make an atonement with him, and to let him go for a scapegoat into the wilderness." (Leviticus 16:10.) After the high priest had performed the sacrifice and sprinkled the blood seven times upon the mercy seat as an atonement for his own sins and those of Israel, he would "lay both his hands upon the head of the live goat, and confess over him all the iniquities of the children of Israel, and all their transgressions in all their sins, putting them upon the head of the goat, and shall send him away . . . into the wilderness." (Leviticus 16:21.) And thus the innocent animal, carrying everyone's burdens of guilt, would wander away in the wilderness to die of starvation and thirst or to fall prey to wild beasts.

I have had a sense that many mothers are wandering in just such a wilderness, burdened with guilt that they have accepted but of which they are innocent. It is true that much is expected of Latter-day Saint women. Mothers bear a great responsibility. But guilt is a burden they need not pick up. They need not make themselves responsible for the deficiencies of society. It is not for them to bear unmerited guilt for divorce, juvenile delinquency, drug abuse, teenage sexuality, theft, and violence. They need to know where they stand in their own eyes and where they stand with the Lord. That precious knowledge is not something they should let someone else decide for them.

Christ died and rose again to free us from burdens. The only burden that he lays upon the women of the Church is the shared yoke he offers every individual—man, woman, and child—who accepts his name in the waters of baptism. It is a "burden" that comes with a promise: "Come unto me, all ye that labour and are heavy laden, and I will give you rest. Take my yoke upon you, and learn of me; for I am meek and lowly in heart: and ye shall find rest unto your souls. For my yoke is easy, and my burden is light." (Matthew 11:28–30.)

CHAPTER EIGHT

# Defining Ourselves

Perhaps you have played the game in which you choose an unfamiliar word from the dictionary and each member of the team composes a definition for it. One person has the real definition. Then each person gives his or her definition, and the other team tries to guess which one is the right one. I'd like to begin this chapter by asking you to guess the definition of the word *eleemosynary*. (No fair pulling out the *Webster's*!) *Eleemosynary*. Here are the definitions:

1. dwelling in mud.
2. supported by charity or the giving of alms.
3. turning or bending into a different position at night.
4. concerned with representing effects of outdoor light and atmosphere.

If you chose the second definition, you're correct, though the other definitions are for real words, too. "Dwelling in mud" is the definition for *limicolous*. "Turning or bending into a different position at night" defines *nyctitropic*. "Concerned with representing effects of outdoor light and atmosphere" defines the *plein-air* school of Impressionist painting.

Definitions are part of everyday life. We're defined by our position in and phase of life, as well as a host of other criteria. Perhaps you share one of my own life's definitions with me — that of being a convert, or of belonging to a part-member family. You may have a husband, parent, sibling, child, or grandchild who isn't a member of the Church.

How do you deal with that? It can be very painful when you, as a family member, make a choice that puts some distance between you and the rest of your family. When I joined the Church at age fifteen, I was lucky. I was living away from home. I had been attending church since I was eleven, when the missionaries had begun holding a religion class not far from the school during my study period. I was fascinated. I loved Sunday School. I loved singing the hymns with those wonderful Hawaiian members who were so good to me. My parents did not mind that I was involved with this American religion, for Buddhism does not place exclusive demands on its adherents. Monthly, I attended prayer services in our local temple with my parents and followed the usual observances at the family shrine. So for four years, I was both a Buddhist and a Mormon. Finally, at age fifteen, I was baptized. If my parents had not had four years of seeing my involvement with the Church, they would have been upset; but they already knew that I could be a good Mormon and a good daughter, so there was no upheaval in the family.

It was different for my husband. When he met me, he had a good definition of his life already. He was a devoted Congregationalist, just back from a year's recuperation in Battle Creek, Michigan, from a wound suffered in France during World War II. Because of the interruption of the war, we were both sophomores at the University of Hawaii.

I liked who Ed was. I liked the definitions he had of himself. I seriously considered whether our definitions would match. I thought long and hard about our relationship as it moved from friendship toward love. The options for single Mormon women were very limited in Hawaii then. I knew that I faced a choice between marrying out of the Church or, very probably, never marrying. I prayed earnestly. I could feel and see greatness in Ed. He had a Christian heart. He scrupulously lived every

principle of the gospel that he had learned as a Congregationalist and found joy in doing so. I had great faith that he was
an honest man and would accept greater truth when he was
able to learn about it. And if he did not, I felt that we could
still have a good Christian marriage, based on mutual respect
for each other's beliefs, a desire to serve others, and the strong
love that I already felt between us.

So we married, and Ed was baptized ten months later. It
was devastating to his mother. He was the oldest son, and his
father was dead. That meant, according to Japanese culture,
that he was responsible for her care. Social stratification went
along with church attendance in Hawaii. Caucasian Americans
attended their own chapel in the Congregational Church. Educated professionals from Japanese families attended the
Union Church, also a Congregational unit. Ed and I both were
professionals—I was a teacher and he was a court probation
officer. His mother was pleased with that. I was a suitable
match for him in education.

But not religiously. On the third level were churches that
weren't as "respectable" somehow. Pentecostal and evangel-
ical groups. And the Mormons. The plantation workers, ditch-
diggers, and unskilled laborers attended that church. Suddenly
Ed was attending this "lower-class" church with me and em-
barrassing the family when, according to the rules of Japanese
culture, the wife should conform to the husband's social class.

You can imagine what a shock this was for Ed's mother.
She had a clear definition of who Ed was and what our marriage
should be like—those traditional definitions that came from
our culture. I tried to fit her definition as much as I could. I
had seen how anxious my mother had been about being a good
daughter-in-law, and I also worked hard to be a good daughter-
in-law. We spent as much time with Ed's family as we could.
I was always solicitous about his mother's welfare and called

her two or three times a week. I always tried to be helpful and pleasant to her.

But she could see that Ed was moving away from the place in the family that she wanted him to occupy. His extended family always gathered at his grandmother's house on Sundays and spent the day playing poker, eating, drinking coffee, and visiting. But as Ed became interested and involved in the Church, his definition of himself and his role in the family began to change. Ed and I could spend only parts of Sundays with his extended family because we were attending church. And then Ed stopped drinking coffee. And then he stopped playing poker. And then his mother found out that he was giving 10 percent of his money to this unrespectable church. It was just one thing after another. When Ed was baptized, his mother was so angry that she stopped speaking to him. In fact, she didn't communicate with him for twenty years.

This was a painful time for us both. Things might have been different if we had stayed in Hawaii, but Ed used the G.I. Bill to finish his master's degree at the University of Utah, and we didn't have the money to return to Hawaii for many years. Fortunately, Ed's mother was financially well off, so he didn't have to worry about her economic needs.

We stayed in touch, but it was very lopsided communication for those twenty years. We wrote regularly. We sent photos of our sons, Christmas cards, and presents for his mother's birthday and Christmas—but she never answered. Fortunately, Ed's brother and sister kept in touch, so we knew that Ed's mother read the letters, even if she wouldn't answer them. What finally broke the ice was when Ed was called to preside over the Japan Okinawa Mission. As it turned out, Ed's sister-in-law had joined the Church and told his mother, "Hey, this is really a big deal! Ed is very important." So his mother came to visit us in Japan. Ed took her to visit the family shrine at Yanai and collected family genealogy with her. They were able to bridge that silence of twenty years. I think having the two grandsons there helped a lot, too.

From that point on, whenever Ed went to Hawaii he received the prodigal son treatment. His brother and sister would tease him that he couldn't do anything wrong. And his mother thinks I'm the best daughter-in-law in the world. Her definitions of us and our definitions of ourselves finally accommodated each other. I don't know if she'll ever join the Church, and she made Ed promise that he would never have ordinances performed in behalf of his deceased father. But at least we're friendly now. My own parents were never hostile about the Church, so it was never hard for me. But I'm still the only member of the Church in my family.

Now, the point I want to make is this: Ed was trying to be the best son, the best son-in-law, and the best Mormon he could be. I was trying to be the best daughter, daughter-in-law, and Mormon I could be. Those were three role definitions apiece we were trying to work out with our families and the Church—not to mention trying to be the best husband and wife to each other we could be. How we succeeded had a large impact on our self-esteem. But there came a point where we had to choose. Ed couldn't be the best son—in terms of Japanese culture and in terms of what his mother wanted—and also be the best Mormon he could be. I couldn't be the best daughter-in-law—in terms of what his mother wanted—and still be the best Mormon I could be. Being a good daughter-in-law was important to me, but being a good Mormon was more important. Being a good son was important to Ed, but being a good Mormon was more important. So he had to establish that definition of himself without knowing if his mother would ever come to terms with it.

I feel so grateful that we made the same decision and that we could make it together. What if Ed had felt that it was more important for him to please his mother than to be a good Mormon? What would that have done to our marriage? I know that we're a lot luckier and a lot more blessed than many, many people who are struggling with circumstances much like ours. But even if one of us had made a different decision, I think we still could have made the marriage work. There just would have been something important missing from our relationship—something that we couldn't fully share.

For both of us, the religious principles we had learned in our homes and in our former religious traditions were beautiful and solid parts of our foundation. Understanding the plan of salvation, knowing our true relationship to our Father in heaven, and feeling the love of Jesus and the power of his atoning sacrifice were beautiful parts of the gospel that made us feel like new people. I love the scripture in 2 Corinthians where Paul explains this new life: "[Christ] died for all, that those who live should no longer live for themselves but for him who died for them and was raised again. So from now on we regard no one from a worldly point of view. Though we once regarded Christ in this way, we do so no longer. Therefore, if anyone is in Christ, [she] is a new creation; the old has gone, the new has come!" (NIV, 2 Corinthians 5:15–17.)

Do you feel that newness? Do you feel that strong connection to Jesus and the love that he has for you? If you do, it makes it easy to choose being a good member of the Church first.

How, though, do we put the Savior first without putting down other people or their religions? We don't have to insist on being right all the time. When my parents drank tea, I sat with them and drank hot water. Make compromises. Find ways to serve. Minimize the areas of conflict. Don't retaliate. After all, you want your family to see that you're a better, happier person as a result of belonging to the Church.

Be spiritually independent enough that your relationship with the Savior doesn't depend on your circumstances or on what other people say and do. Have the spiritual independence to be a Mormon—the best Mormon you can—in your own way. Not the bishop's way. Not the Relief Society president's way. Your way.

Consider this statement by a woman who felt she didn't fit the Relief Society president mold at all—but somehow managed to serve anyway. Cathy Stokes is a black woman, a former Baptist, a single mother, and had been a convert of four years when she was called to be Relief Society president of the Hyde Park Ward in the Chicago Heights, Illinois, Stake. This ward specialized in diversity: "The men in the ward speak German, Japanese, Italian, Swedish, and several varieties of English." Membership among the sisters ranges from the vice-president of a university to students of that same university. Some families have been in the Church for many generations; others are converts. When she was called, Cathy says, "My daughter's reaction was, 'They have made a *serious* mistake. You don't have a bouffant hairdo, and you don't do Jello. And besides,' she said, 'Relief Society presidents smile all the time and have to take everything. You may smile, but you don't take *anything* from *anyone*. This is not going to work.'

"While I was turning my calling over in my mind and struggling to understand it, I got an answer to my question in the form of a song. An old spiritual says, 'There's plenty good room, Plenty good room, Plenty good room in my Father's kingdom. There's plenty good room, Plenty good room, So choose your seat and sit down.' " ("Plenty Good Room in Relief Society," *Dialogue*, Winter 1988, p. 84.)

There *is* plenty of room—room for us all. In many ways, we need to be each other's families. And the one thing about a family is that you belong to it just by being born. In the Church, that birth is our baptism. Relief Society should be a society of sisters, not a place where you have to watch what you say, or bite your tongue all the way through a meeting.

Part of our spiritual independence is simply shaking off wrongful messages about who we are. We get them from people who don't know us but who judge us, from people who restrict us from being who we are. Jesus sees you as you are and knows you to the very foundation of your being and loves you enough that he died for you—more than that, came alive again for you.

I keep struggling toward the Father's perspective of mortality. Every now and then I catch a glimpse of things from his perspective. Such glimpses give me strength; they fill me with courage; they replenish my gratitude to overflowing. See yourself as the Father sees you—glorious, eternal, capable of infinite love, worthy of *his* infinite love.

The Apostle Peter, in his first epistle to the Saints in the northern part of Asia Minor, opens his letter with this same vision of courage, comfort, and strength: Praise be to the God and Father of our Lord Jesus Christ! In his great mercy he has given us new birth into a living hope through the resurrection of Jesus Christ from the dead, and into an inheritance that can never perish, spoil or fade—kept in heaven for you. . . . In this you greatly rejoice, though now for a little while you may have had to suffer grief in all kinds of trials. These have come so that your faith—of greater worth than gold, which perishes even though refined by fire—may be proved genuine and may result in praise, glory and honor when Jesus Christ is revealed." (NIV, 1 Peter 1:3–7.)

Isn't that a wonderful idea? The Father has given us an inheritance in heaven that will never perish, spoil, or fade. It's there for us right now! We can rejoice in it right now! Yes, we have problems and trials. Yes, we may suffer grief. But these trials will prove that our faith is genuine. Notice that Peter doesn't threaten the Saints ("you'd better pass this test!") or sound anxious ("oh, dear, I hope you can pass this test!"). Instead he assures them that their faith will be proved genuine and will increase the "praise, glory, and honor" that will greet our Savior when Jesus returns a second time to the earth.

Then Peter writes so tenderly, so consolingly, so comfortingly that his words are an embrace of love. He reminds the Saints of their faith and bears testimony with them and for them in words of power, love, and exultation. In this he speaks for us, the Saints of the latter-day church, as well: "Though you have not seen him, you love him; and even though you do not see him now, you believe in him and are filled with an inexpressible and glorious joy, for you are receiving the goal of your faith, the salvation of your souls. . . . Even angels long to look into these things." (NIV, 1 Peter 1:8–9, 12.)

CHAPTER NINE

# Three Ideas for a Brighter Life

AT THE RISK OF IMPLYING THAT IT IS possible to reduce a successful life formula to a few points, let me suggest three ideas to make life easier to live. The first is permission to make mistakes. The second is the ability to accept what life has to give. And the third is a stronger trust in the Savior.

PERMISSION TO MAKE MISTAKES

Let's talk first about mistakes. I'm a teacher, and I know from firsthand observation that one of the most important things a teacher can do in creating an environment for learning is to give children permission to make mistakes.

When I was teaching second grade in Salt Lake City many years ago, one of the biggest hurdles of the year was subtraction—which can be a pretty abstract concept if you don't have a clear idea about number value. One little guy—I'll call him Loren—just seemed traumatized by it. He would listen anxiously to the explanation and watch the demonstration with his eyes riveted on the blackboard. But when it was time to start doing the problems on the page in front of him, his face would crumple, his eyes would fill with tears, and he would dissolve in sobs.

On the first day, I thought he was just having a bad day. On the second day, I thought he hadn't understood the concept. But on the third day, I realized that we had a problem. So on the fourth day, I whispered to him at the beginning of class, before we even started the day's exercises, "Now I want you to do something for me, Loren. As soon as you feel tears coming, will you quickly raise this finger?" I tapped the index finger on his left hand. "Raise it very quickly and the tears won't come, but *I* will come. Okay?"

So he did. The first day, he raised his finger as soon as he'd written down the problem. I came immediately to his side, praised how well he'd written the numbers, and sat with him as he wrote down the answer. "That was fine, Loren!" I said. "Now next time, write down the problem *and* the answer before you raise your finger." So he did. By the end of class, he was working three problems at a time before the tears rose up.

And so we kept on, day after day. And after a week, Loren was working serenely away at the same rate as the other children. Now the interesting point is that he knew how to do subtraction. He was not having trouble with the concept. He very seldom made a mistake. But it was the fear of making a mistake that paralyzed him, traumatized him, and made him dissolve in tears.

Does that happen to us sometimes? Are we so frightened by the possibility of making a mistake that we can't even get started? Does the idea of trying something new seem so scary that the very thought makes panicky feelings rise in our throat? Well, just pick up a pencil. Which end is the important end? They both are! Sometimes the writing end is important and sometimes the erasing end is important, depending on what you just did and what you want to do in the next few minutes. Does the pencil care? Certainly not! It's happy that both ends will be used.

An old proverb states: "He who makes no mistakes does not usually make anything." If we're going to accomplish anything worthwhile, we need to give ourselves permission to make a lot of mistakes!

But what if you've made a serious mistake? What if your exercise of agency has led you into sin? Do you think there's an eraser big enough for you? Perhaps you read an article in the August 1990 *Ensign* about a bishop who was released from his calling and excommunicated for a transgression that he does not specify. I was touched by his account, particularly by two passages in which he describes the love of God:

"[At] times as my soul cries out with a distressed 'Why?' the Lord calms my soul and fills my mind with understanding. At such times, I cannot write the ideas as fast as He gives them to me. He teaches me about sacred covenants and the process of cleansing." Pay attention, now, to this next sentence! "I do not feel chastised or rebuked. I feel taught. I thank Him for his kindness. For His patience. For His love. . . .

"The stake president visits me. 'You're doing well,' he says. 'Don't you feel hopeful now?'

"No. I feel hurt and lost and sad and tragically foolish. But I do sometimes feel loved. I hope that the Lord's love can reach past my persistent weakness and stubbornness and make something of me. It is strange that so many tearful hours can be sweet. But sometimes in the sadness I sense the message that we are strangers here, that He loves us, and that He is waiting at the gate for our return. It is a divine sadness. Sweet. Filled with the longing for home." ("Yearning to Return," *Ensign*, August 1990, p. 24.)

This man had committed a sin, but he was repenting. That's important. And the Lord was not punishing him. The Lord was teaching him and loving him. There was a sweetness in the repentance.

Many times we equate all mistakes with sin. Sin involves two characteristics: knowing the law and willfully breaking the law— in other words, deliberately choosing evil over good when we know what the good is. In many situations, we simply do not know what constitutes good. We have to make choices between two unknowns. We have to choose between two good things, hoping we will benefit from the choice. Or we have to choose between two less-than-desirable alternatives, and hope we have chosen the lesser of two evils. Accepting ambiguity is one of the signs of an adult. We cannot predict the consequences of some choices until after we have made the choice. Sometimes it takes years for us to understand the significance of a choice we have made.

But should we be paralyzed, hesitating between choices, trying to keep all our options open forever? Of course not. Our Heavenly Father floods us with choices that we must make every day — when to get up, what to eat, what to wear, whether to smile or not, what to think about, what to listen to, how to speak to each other. He wants us to practice and practice and practice choosing.

Life isn't a true-false test. It's literally multiple choice. On many of the choices, all of the answers are partially right, but none is completely right. The only way we can get that problem wrong on the test is to leave it blank.

Of course we should get the best information we can. Of course we should think carefully through our options. Of course we should ponder prayerfully to learn the desires of our Heavenly Father. But remember that wonderful scripture from the Doctrine and Covenants: "Wherefore, go ye and preach my gospel, whether to the north or to the south, to the east or to the west, it mattereth not, for ye cannot go amiss." (D&C 80:3.) I want to repeat those last words, because I think they're so important: "it mattereth not, for ye cannot go amiss." Remember, in some cases any choice is the right choice. It just depends on what we make of it.

What are some things in which we "cannot go amiss"? Doing our best. Living the gospel. Being good Christians. We don't need a formal Church calling to have a wonderful relationship with our Father in heaven and to feel happy and committed in service. Once we've stepped out of the waters of baptism, we bear the name of Christ. We don't have to fill out a form and stand in line for it. Once we've been confirmed a member of the Church, we have the gift of the Holy Ghost. We don't have to drive out to the Distribution Center to pick it up. The bishop doesn't have to call us to be a compassionate Christian. We don't have to sign up to be a thoughtful neighbor. The congregation doesn't have to sustain us before we can be kind and sensitive. We don't have to be set apart to love someone. We don't need anyone's permission to do good. We can just go out and do it on our own.

When I was a tiny girl, just old enough to walk, my mother began teaching me a wonderful principle of seeking out good to do. The Japanese word for this self-motivated goodness is *kigatsuku*. When she was sweeping the floor, she would say, "Chieko, what would a *kigatsuku* girl do now?" I would think for a minute, and then run to get the dustpan and hold it for her. Or when she was washing dishes, I would pick up the dish towel and begin to dry them. She would smile and say, "You are a *kigatsuku* girl."

*Kigatsuku* means an inner spirit to act without being told what to do. Years later, I read that beautiful scripture in Doctrine and Covenants 58:27–28 that exactly captures the meaning of *kigatsuku*: "[You] should be anxiously engaged in a good cause, and do many things of [your] own free will, and bring to pass much righteousness; for the power is in [you], wherein [you] are agents unto [yourselves]."

*Kigatsuku* is a principle of enormous power. It taught me that, even as a child, not only could I recognize good without needing someone to tell it to me, but I also had the power to perform good. It taught me trust in my own perception and in

107

my own power. Isn't that *kigatsuku* principle one that's worth learning? There's nothing that automatically brings such happiness as being able to see a real need and perform a real service.

What this principle leads to is developing a Christlike character—through thick and through thin, through mistakes and through successes, through good choices and through bad choices.

## ACCEPTING WHAT LIFE OFFERS

The second idea that will add some brightness and lightness to life is the recommendation that we accept what life has to offer us. Let me relate a Japanese folktale that illustrates this point. It is called *Hanasaka Jijii*, or "The Old Man Who Made Dead Trees Bloom." Pay attention to the reactions of the old man in the story. In this ancient folktale, an old man and woman who were honest and kind-hearted lived next to a wicked and greedy old man.

The kindly couple had adopted a little dog as a pet. This dog led the old man to the garden one day and began barking and scratching at the ground in one certain spot. Perplexed, the old man dug there, and uncovered a treasure of jewels and *oban* and *koban,* coins minted during the feudal period of Japan. The greedy old man from next door happened by as the good couple were exclaiming over the find, and they cheerfully loaned him the dog.

As instructed, the greedy man followed the dog into his own garden and dug where the dog barked and scratched. But instead of riches, he dug up a disgusting nest of frogs, lizards, and reptiles. Angry and frustrated, he killed the little dog and buried it in the garden, marking the spot with a willow twig.

When their pet failed to return, the good old man went to his cruel neighbor and learned what he had done. The next day, he went to the spot where his dog was buried, to console his spirit. Imagine his surprise when he found a giant willow tree growing there! The man chopped down the tree and made a mortar and pestle out of the trunk. He and his wife put steamed rice in the mortar and were pounding it to make *mochi*, rice cakes, when *oban* and *koban* began pouring out.

The greedy neighbor just happened to be peeking in the window at the time, and asked to borrow the mortar and pestle. But as he began pounding the rice, filthy things tumbled out — discarded roof tiles, broken utensils, and the like, but not a glimpse of a gold coin. The infuriated old man threw the mortar and pestle into his kitchen brazier. When his kindly neighbor came to retrieve them, all that was left was a pile of ashes.

Resigned to his loss, the good man gathered up the ashes that had once been his mortar and pestle and started for home. On his way, he spilled some of the ashes onto a spot where green grass had long since withered. Instantly, the grass flowered into fresh green!

With joy, the old man hurried home, climbed a tree in his garden, and sprinkled the ashes all around. All the trees in the neighborhood, even the dead ones, burst out with beautiful blooms. The people all applauded the old man's feat and called him "Hanasaka jijii," which means "Old Man Who Makes Dead Trees Flower."

Look at the different reactions to life that these two men had. The wicked neighbor was never anything but selfish, jealous, ungenerous, and greedy. The good old man genuinely sorrowed over the grievous things that happened to him, but he did not retaliate or seek revenge. Nor did he pretend that what had happened wasn't bad. In other words, there was no false cheerfulness or mere Pollyanna optimism here. No denial. But there was no rejection or anger, either. He mourned over the grave of his little dog and went back to "console his spirit," rather than going out to buy a new dog or just staying away

109

from the painful reminder. He embraced the tree that grew from the grave and turned it into the mortar and pestle that produced the stream of coins. Now, cutting down a tree and carving a mortar and pestle are a long process. But he was prepared to invest the time in this important project and, as a result, something miraculous happened.

When the evil old man burned the mortar, again the good old man did not pretend it was all right. He knew it was wrong and evil. He grieved. But he picked up the ashes—which were all that was left—and again something wonderful and magical happened, and the dead trees began to flower.

In other words, the good old man did not reject what confronted him. He grieved for what was gone but accepted what was there.

Life often treats us the way it did the good old man. When our little dog dies, we want our dog back. We go to the grave and mourn. But if our broken heart can be comforted only by the dog, then sometimes we fail to see the willow tree growing from the grave. Sometimes we try to replace the dog. We spend the next ten years buying puppy after puppy, wondering why we can't find the perfect replacement for our little dog. Well, I think one of the reasons we fail in this is that we aren't the same person anymore as the person who has lost the dog. The experience of having and loving and losing the dog changes us from the person who originally had the dog. Life is ready to grow us a willow tree, but if we can't see it, we'll never be able to carve out our mortar and pestle. Let's accept what life offers us. Maybe it looks like a handful of ashes. But let's pick up that handful and see what we can do with it.

## DEVELOP TRUST IN THE LORD

The third idea to increase brightness and lightness in our lives is to develop more trust in the Savior and in his love for each one of us. Remember where the Apostle Paul says, "Who shall separate us from the love of Christ? shall tribulation, or distress, or persecution, or famine, or nakedness, or peril, or sword? . . . Nay, in all these things we are more than conquerors through him that loved us." (Romans 8:35, 37.)

Do you sometimes have difficulty believing that Christ really died for *you?* That he really loves *you?* We all have moments when that seems impossible and incredible. Why is it so hard for us to believe the good news of the gospel when it's so easy for us to believe bad news? I think this must be something of a universal problem.

John Bunyan had this problem. He was a Separatist minister in England during the seventeenth century, and you may recognize him as the author of *Pilgrim's Progress,* but you may not know that he also wrote a wonderful spiritual autobiography called *Grace Abounding* in 1666. In it he tells how he felt condemned by his own conscience, feeling that he was such a great sinner: "I felt my heart sink in despair, concluding it was too late; and so I decided that I might as well go on in sin." (*Grace Abounding to the Chief of Sinners* [Chicago: Moody Bible Institute, 1959], p. 13.) Do you sometimes feel like that?

He recounts many experiences during his spiritual quest that finally convinced him Jesus was truly his Savior. In one example, he felt it would do him no good to pray, but he forced himself to do it anyway. While he was praying, he says, a scripture from Matthew came to him: " 'O . . . great is thy faith.' This came to me as sharply and suddenly as though someone had slapped me on the back while I was there on my knees, yet I was not able to believe that this was a prayer of faith. . . . I just could not believe it."

A second example occurred a few days later while "[I] was desperately debating . . . whether . . . Christ was sufficient to save my soul, I was quite worn out with my fears [when] suddenly the words, 'He is able' came into my heart. It seemed that these words were spoken aloud to me, and all fear was knocked out of me for at least a day; I had never had more certainty in my life."

A third experience came when he was in church: "I was full of sadness and terror, for my fears were strong upon me. Suddenly there broke in upon me this word, 'My grace is sufficient for thee, My grace is sufficient for thee, My grace is sufficient for thee.' Three times it came. The word was a mighty one . . . I felt as though I had seen the Lord Jesus looking down from heaven right through the roof, directing his words right to me. This sent me home . . . filled with joy." (*Grace Abounding*, pp. 72–74.)

So he began to understand and accept that the atonement of Christ applied to him. At this point, reading the scriptures became sweet to him, and he said, "I tried to take the words as God had laid them down without trying to explain away a single syllable of them. I began to realize that God had a bigger mouth to speak with than I had a heart to understand. I realized also that He had not spoken His words hastily but with infinite wisdom and judgement, and in very truth and faithfulness." (P. 86.) Isn't that a beautiful way to feast on the scriptures? He also said, and this is important, "It was not my good feelings that made my righteousness better, and . . . my bad feelings did not make my righteousness worse; for my righteousness was Jesus Christ Himself, 'the same yesterday, and today, and forever.' " (Pp. 80–81.)

Perhaps you've had an experience like John Bunyan's. If you have, hold to it fiercely. Don't let it go. And if you haven't, don't give up. Someday we will all know who we are, because the Savior, who truly knows us, will look at us and we will see ourselves through his eyes — pure, eternal, and all-knowing —

rather than through our own mortal, shortsighted, dim perspective. And when we see ourselves as he sees us, we will recognize our glory.

Remember these three ideas for a brighter life: First, you have permission to make mistakes. Second, accept what life gives you. And third, trust in the Lord's love for you. I do. He is my rock and my salvation, my wings and my roots.

# Embracing Charity

CHAPTER TEN

# The Pure Spirit of Charity

I ONCE ATTENDED A welfare meeting in which many policies
and procedures were discussed. President Gordon B. Hinckley,
who was present but not conducting, listened quietly for much
of the meeting. When the conducting officer, near the end of
the meeting, asked if he had anything to say, he replied, "No,
I think everything has been said," hesitated a moment, then
said with sudden energy, "Wait. I do have something to say.
And that is: Let us remember, in all we do, the spirit of the
Savior."

It was a simple phrase, but it sliced through what had seemed
to be a complicated and overwhelming procedure. The internal
struggle I had been having to be fair, prudent, and economical —
which had created such worry in me during the meeting
suddenly smoothed itself out in my mind as I visualized the
Savior, not administering a complicated program but tenderly
ministering to one individual at a time.

I greatly appreciated President Hinckley's clarity of focus on
the spirit of the Savior, on what was involved in the practice
of pure charity. The promise of the Book of Mormon thrills
me: "Charity is the pure love of Christ, and it endureth forever;
and whoso is found possessed of it at the last day, it shall be
well with him. Wherefore, my beloved brethren, pray unto the
Father with all the energy of heart, that ye may be filled with
this love, which he hath bestowed upon all who are true followers of his Son, Jesus Christ." (Moroni 7:47–48.)

As I have thought about this passage and its meaning in my life, I have found two other parts that speak deeply to me. One is the commandment to "cleave unto charity," and the other is the promise that, if we are endowed with charity, "we shall be like" Jesus Christ when he appears, for we "may be purified even as he is pure." (Moroni 7:46, 48.)

But what is charity, that pure and purifying spirit of love? What does it mean in our lives—or what should it mean? I have a brisk and somewhat practical turn of mind, I would say. I am not by nature contemplative or mystical. It is easy for me to grasp rules of behavior, to manage procedures, to work out policies, to set specific goals and to achieve them. And so I have had to struggle and grope for the vision behind these words. I believe that I have felt Christ's pure love for me from time to time, sometimes when I have been engaged in his work, but sometimes for no reason that I could identify, simply as a great wave of pure feeling that I have accepted as a grace and as a blessing.

There is no way, of course, of controlling such gifts or of having them available on demand. But I have noticed there are some things I can do that help me feel purer, more ready to receive the gift. These are actions—disciplines, if you will—that seem to keep me focused on the spirit of charity, just as President Hinckley's remark refocused our attention back on the spirit that should motivate our efforts in that welfare meeting. First, I can make a conscious effort to avoid being judgmental about others and their actions. Second, I can earnestly seek to look on the "inward" person, to see spirit and heart rather than externals. Third, I can seek opportunities to be actively engaged in serving others.

AVOID JUDGMENTS

I recall driving to work one morning with my mind turning over the very concept of being judgmental. A recent Relief Society lesson had focused my attention on this principle, and I had realized that although I was generally relaxed about people and enjoyed the individual patterns in their behavior, I often summed them up quietly to myself or made judgments about their motives.

This particular morning, while I was waiting for a traffic light to change, I glanced at the car next to me and saw that the woman who was driving had taken advantage of the momentary halt to hurriedly apply mascara. The light changed and the traffic moved forward. She was driving with one hand, still hastily dabbing on eye shadow with her gaze fixed on the mirror as her car moved into the intersection. I instantly thought, "Oh my goodness! She's going to cause an accident. Why on earth doesn't she just get up ten minutes earlier?"

Then I realized what I was doing and almost laughed at myself. Here I was, instantly leaping to the conclusion that she had been undisciplined and careless with her time. I didn't know her circumstances. I didn't know what kind of morning she had had. For all I knew she had been up for hours, working to prepare breakfast and lunches for four or five children and get them happily off to school, caring for everybody else before she thought of herself.

Tiny though that incident was, I have never forgotten it. It reminds me that when I construct such a scenario—seeing an action and instantly assuming that I understand the motives behind it—I limit my ability to reach out in fellowship or helpfulness. Such judgmental thinking contaminates the purity of whatever charity I may be feeling and removes me, by so much, from the spirit of Christ and his own pure love.

I take this judgment upon myself seriously, so I know how grateful I have been when others have withheld judgment and have given me a chance to prove myself as an individual.

SEEK TO PERCEIVE THE INNER PERSON

The second thing we can do to purify ourselves to better receive the gift of Christ's love is to seek to perceive what a person's spirit is like, to look past externals to the true core and center of a person. I have always believed that people are basically good and that they want to do good and to be good. Often they need help in finding better ways of acting on the feelings toward goodness that they have inside, and this is the wondrousness of the gospel—that it helps all of us find ways to express and refine our desires for goodness.

I have always loved the story of Samuel and David in the Old Testament when Samuel, following the Lord's instructions to anoint a new king for Israel, went to the house of Jesse and looked at his seven stalwart sons. "Surely," he thought, upon seeing the eldest, "the Lord's anointed is before [me]." But the spirit of the Lord instructed him in a divine perspective, "Look not on his countenance, or on the height of his stature; . . . for the Lord seeth not as a man seeth; for man looketh on the outward appearance, but the Lord looketh on the heart." (1 Samuel 16:6–7.)

Have you desired and sought for the gift of looking beyond the outward appearance and perceiving the heart of an individual? Looking toward the heart is a skill we can acquire. The Spirit will reveal to us what the spirit of another individual is like, no matter how the outward appearance may initially strike us. What if I had not been able to look into Ed's heart during our courtship when I had to ponder seriously the potential consequences of marrying someone who was not a Mormon? I might have hesitated out of fear and lost a great companion on life's journey, one who has brought a merry and a tender heart to our home as my husband and as the father of our children. I simply cannot imagine what my life would have been like without Ed's enthusiasm, his joy, and his strong commitment to the gospel.

Ed and I had many wonderful opportunities to serve, and sometimes we were "firsts": Ed was the first of Japanese ancestry to be a home service director for Utah's Red Cross and later became its first state director of aging. He was the second man of Japanese ancestry to be called as a mission president. (Elder Adney Y. Komatsu was the first.) There had been a few other teachers of Japanese ancestry in Salt Lake City, but I became the first exchange teacher from Hawaii to teach there. Later I was the first principal of Japanese ancestry at Cherry Creek District in Aurora, Colorado, where we spent many years. I was the first non-Caucasian called to any general board when Florence Jacobsen, the YWMIA general president, asked me to serve in 1961. When President Ezra Taft Benson, then an apostle, set me apart in 1961 for the YWMIA, he told me I was a "pioneer." Later, I became the first woman of Japanese ancestry to serve on the Primary general board, and I am the first non-Caucasian to serve in the Relief Society general presidency.

We have been grateful for all of these opportunities, have tried to do our best in them, and have supported each other in our positions. But as any leader knows, there can be no leadership without fellowship, and so we have always been grateful, too, for those who have sustained us in these positions. Often it must have been a bit difficult for people to see past the ways we may have seemed different from them, and I was always grateful when they looked at our hearts instead. I can truly say that once we understood each other's spirits, no external difference had any importance.

I remember during the 1960s when Ed and I were in Japan on our mission. Some "hippies" began attending services in the Abeno Branch in Osaka. Some of our faithful elders, who knew the efforts Brigham Young University made to uphold its dress code and the heroic efforts of bishops to persuade their wards' young people not to follow these worldly trends, were concerned about the presence of these people with their long hair, beads, and shabby blue jeans. Were they really ready for the gospel? Wouldn't they set a bad example to Church members?

I reminded the elders of the scripture from 1 Samuel that told them to look on the heart, then said: "The important thing is that they are here. As long as they are here, you can teach them. The Spirit will tell them when it is time to wear different clothes or to cut their hair; but until their hearts change, none of that is important." Not all of the investigators who visited our meetings were baptized, of course, and our "hippies" were no exception. But among those who stayed, learned the gospel, and were converted, it was soon impossible to tell any difference—external or internal—between them and long-time members.

## DIFFERENCES—JUST DIFFERENCES

In Hawaii, I was surrounded from babyhood by differences— in language, in physical appearance, in dress, in economic level, in religion, in traditional men's and women's roles, in education, in race, in life-styles, and in customs. I observed differences, but I did not learn to label them as "good" or "bad." They were just "different." This has been an enormous advantage to me. I have seen elementary school children encountering their first black or handicapped person in the third, fourth, or fifth grade and finding the difference alarming. They label the difference "wrong" or "bad" and find ways to reduce their fear of it by mocking or excluding the different child. It is hard work to take down barriers. In the case of adults, the perception and fear of differences can build barriers so high and tight that they can be permanently crippling. (See Romans 8:15.)

I used to help one of my teachers, a Chinese woman, chop ingredients for stir-fry for her parties; I also learned how to make sponge cake, at which she was an artist. Again, these were differences I filed away. I sometimes attended church with Hawaiians, enjoying the rich harmonies of the Congregationalist hymns they sang in their open Hawaiian syllables. More differences!

Differences, all differences. Not good differences or bad differences, just differences. Being different, I internalized, is all right. Heavenly Father wants differences. He does not make two identical blossoms or two snowflakes that are the same.

As a teacher, I could tell the very first day of class each year which children I could love instantly and which child might be difficult. In each classroom there was always one to whom I was not instinctively drawn. I learned that I must go immediately to that child and return to him or her often during the day—to give a hug, to ruffle up his hair, to pat her shoulder. If I would do that, by day's end, whatever in me sensed a difficult difference about that child had dissolved, and we had created the special bond that had come spontaneously with the others.

I have always tried to seek the good in others and to do good to others. For me, an important part of that has been refusing to label differences as either good or bad, but looking beyond them. It is immensely freeing to be able to say, "Well, they're doing such and such. That's different from the way I would do it, but that's their way." If you think of a difference as bad, there are fewer options in dealing with the person. Nearly always the tendency is to try to change that person so that the difference "disappears"; or else we try to ignore that person so that the difference "goes away." Neither way works very well. I have wondered sometimes if Paul was trying to get the Galatians to see beyond differences of religion, social status, and gender when he wrote, "There is neither Jew nor Greek, there is neither bond nor free, there is neither male nor female: for ye are all one in Christ Jesus." (Galatians 3:28.)

SEEKING OPPORTUNITIES FOR SERVICE

Another important part of being pure enough to receive the pure love of Christ is seeking opportunities for service. As I mentioned previously, as a *kigatsuku* girl, I would get the dustpan and help my mother, or get a dishtowel and help her dry the dishes, or start rinsing the clothes as she scrubbed them on a board. I learned to see what needed to be done. I learned to act without waiting for either invitations or instructions.

We were put here on the earth to do good. In the gospel, there are many things that become unimportant if our "eye is single" to the task of building the kingdom. I felt a particular responsibility in Japan where the members and investigators watched us closely. Ed and I used to laugh; in the United States, we felt like Americans but people expected us to behave like Japanese because that's how we looked. In Japan, we looked Japanese so we often surprised people with our Americanism. But in both places it was the "Mormon way" that we tried to exemplify.

For example, women in traditional Japanese society are expected to be retiring and inconspicuous in public life, and some of the members in Japan interpreted their understanding of the priesthood in a way that reinforced this traditional concept. Because I was president of all of the auxiliaries in the mission, my husband asked me to attend all the mission presidency meetings with his two Japanese counselors, both to explain about the work of the auxiliaries and to take minutes. After one of the first meetings, one counselor protested, "President, this is a priesthood meeting. A woman should not be in attendance." Ed had expected this point to come up, so he was prepared and explained calmly, "The work of the mission cannot be done if the auxiliaries are not working. Do you understand that work? Can you teach us about them?" The brother admitted he could not. So Ed summed up, "The work of the mission requires everyone: missionaries who hold the priesthood and missionaries who do not, priesthood quorums, and auxiliaries. As long as I am mission president, the president of the auxiliaries will be part of our meetings."

After the initial shock, things were fine. The district auxiliary presidents saw me speaking to congregations of both men and women, asking questions in leadership meetings, sharing information, and giving instructions. So they followed that example and, because of the example Ed and his counselors had set, the women were included as full partners in the district leadership meetings. It was a joy to see the sisters greet my husband, not with a deferential bow and shy silence, but with a smile, a handshake, and all of the news, questions, and information they had to give him. I saw the branches grow sturdy and strong enough to support the leap in baptisms from eighteen the first month we were there to more than two hundred a month.

I remember the groundbreaking for our chapel in Yanai near Hiroshima. The members were struggling to put up a tent for the meeting, but the wind was high and kept snatching at the fabric, toppling the center pole before it could be firmly anchored. When Ed saw this, he instantly dropped his books and briefcase, leaped at the pole, and helped to hold it firm until it could be anchored. Some of the members were scandalized, and one rebuked him, "You should not do this. You are president of the Church in Japan. It is not seemly." Ed said, "My title may be president, but that only means that I am the Lord's servant here in Japan." This was a great lesson to the members.

When the boys and I would come to the Okamachi Chapel to sand benches and sweep floors, the members learned it was not undignified to do that. I still remember our home teacher telling us with awe that he had seen Elder Bernard P. Brockbank, president of the Mormon Pavilion at Expo 1970 in Osaka, down on his knees with a metal scraper digging gum off the carpet after the pavilion had closed one night. "If one of the General Authorities would do that," he said, "then who am I to decide that I am too good for any of the tasks in the Church?"

It is a lesson we all must learn, I think. The important thing is the task. A good deed or a necessary task never complains because the "wrong person" does it. From the task's perspective, the important thing is getting it done.

For all of us, the moments of feeling the pure love of Christ may be rarer than we like. For me, such moments are literally food for my spirit. I can feel the hunger in me when my spirit is not nourished. It is a hunger and thirst for righteousness, and the scriptures tell us we are "blessed" when we feel that hunger and thirst, for we "shall be filled." (Matthew 5:6.) I know of nothing that can more effectively give us the courage to keep on serving when the world seems full of selfishness, to keep praying when the world seems to be brimming with evil, and to keep striving to bring light into a universe that is heavy with darkness.

I love the story that Loren Eiseley tells about the beach of Costabel where shell collectors gather after storms. "Nothing screams but the gulls," he writes, but the beach is one endless scene of death with the starfish slowly strangling in the sand and the "vulturine" collectors throwing the living shellfish into large boiling vats provided by the hotel so that the guests can take away clean shells.

As Eiseley walked this beach at a dark time of his life, feeling neither hope nor pity for the weight of his own blackness, he saw "a gigantic rainbow of incredible perfection" rising over the beach, and at its foot stood a man who stooped, picked up something from the sand, then flung the object far into the surf. When Eiseley came up to him, he found that the man was seeking starfish who were still struggling against the stifling mud. It seemed futile to him, and he walked away; but as he turned and looked back, "for a moment, in the changing light, the sower appeared magnified, as though casting larger stars upon some greater sea."

The image of the star thrower did not leave him. That night Eiseley faced a universe that seemed devoid of human meaning, one moving irresistibly toward decay and death, one in which the Darwinian formula of survival of the species seemed to explain everything about it. But against that bleak and hopeless vision, he saw the star thrower, a human being, stoop and pick up a starfish and throw it back into the sea, native element to the starfish but alien and fatal to the star thrower. He saw that gesture as "an expression of love projected beyond the species boundary." The rainbow under which the star thrower stooped and flung in his tireless work of love was "the circle of perfection . . . toward which the [human] mind had striven."

Eiseley went out on the beach again the next morning. The star thrower was there, but Eiseley did not join him. Instead, he himself began seeking the starfish still living in the puddles and mud at his feet, picked them up, and "flung and flung again while all about us roared the insatiable waters of death. . . . We, pale and alone and small in that immensity, hurled back the living stars. Somewhere far off, across bottomless abysses, I felt as though another world was flung more joyfully. I could have thrown in a frenzy of joy, but I set my shoulders and cast, as the thrower in the rainbow cast, slowly, deliberately, and well. . . . For a moment, we cast on an infinite beach together beside an unknown hurler of suns. . . . Perhaps he smiled and cast once more into the boundless pit of darkness." ("The Star Thrower," in *The Unexpected Universe* [New York: Harcourt Brace Jovanovich, 1964], pp. 69, 71–72, 89–91.)

Loren Eiseley writes of "an unknown hurler of suns." President Hinckley spoke of "the spirit of the Savior." I believe that they are both the same and touch the same chord in us. When we choose mercy, love, and pity, we are choosing order over chaos, life over death. No act of compassion is ever futile or wasted. Each choice to act from tenderness feeds our own spirits and becomes a conduit by which the pure love of Christ can spill into a world hungry for such transforming, abounding, infinite love. We may be ordinary people—vessels made of ordinary clay. But when we experience even a touch of that pure love of Christ, we also experience that promised purity. I have felt something of that transforming power and with it a little—a little that leaves me hungry for more—of the reshaping of our spirits to bear his "eternal weight of glory." (D&C 63:66.)

May we hunger and thirst for it until, in the Lord's due time, we are filled.

# CHAPTER ELEVEN

# Surrounded by Samaritans

ONE OF THE GREATEST LESSONS the Savior taught is that boundaries exist to be crossed. Consider the familiar story of the Good Samaritan, this version taken from a modern translation:

Then a certain teacher of the Law came up and tried to trap Jesus. "Teacher," he asked, "what must I do to receive eternal life?"

Jesus answered him, "What do the Scriptures say? How do you interpret them?" [These are two important questions! It's not enough to know what the scriptures say. We must also think about how we interpret them.]

The man answered, "You must love the Lord your God with all your heart, and with all your soul, and with all your strength, and with all your mind"; and "You must love your neighbor as yourself."

"Your answer is correct," replied Jesus. "Do this, and you will live."

But the teacher of the Law wanted to put himself in the right, so he asked Jesus, "Who is my neighbor?"

Jesus answered: "A certain man was going down from Jerusalem to Jericho, when robbers attacked him, stripped him and beat him up, leaving him half dead. It so happened that a priest was going down that road; when he saw the man he walked on by, on the other side. In the same way, a Levite also came there, went over and looked at the man, and then walked on by, on the other side. But a certain Samaritan who was traveling that way came upon him, and when he saw the man, his heart was filled with pity. He went over to him, poured oil and wine on his wounds and bandaged them; then he put the man on his own animal and took him to an inn, where he took care of him.

"The next day he took out two silver coins and gave them to the innkeeper. 'Take care of him,' he told the innkeeper, 'and when I come back this way I will pay you back whatever you spend on him.'

And Jesus concluded, "Which one of these three seems to you to have been a neighbor to the man attacked by the robbers?"

The teacher of the Law answered, "The one who was kind to him." Jesus replied, "You go, then, and do the same." (Luke 10:26–37, Good News Version [New York: American Bible Society, 1966].)

It never ceases to amaze me how relevant this parable is for our time. The marvel of a parable is that it's a different story if you put yourself in the place of the various people in it. Usually, we think of ourselves as the Good Samaritan, generously helping someone in need. But are there times when we've been the victim who fell among thieves and was left wounded by the wayside? I'm not necessarily thinking about the attack of literal thieves. Sometimes we're victimized by circumstances—such as a flood, a fire, or an automobile accident. Sometimes we're innocent bystanders in someone else's disaster—for example, having parents who were alcoholic or abusive. Sometimes age or poverty or illness leave us helpless by the side of the road. If this has happened to us, has there been a Samaritan for us? Have we been a Samaritan for someone else?

Now think of the story from the perspective of the priest and the Levite. Have there been times when we have seen a need but hurried on by? We may have been frightened and felt the job required more courage than we had. Or maybe we felt awkward and didn't know quite how to offer a helping hand. Or perhaps we felt that the little help we had to offer could not possibly be enough. So we went on, but carried away a burden of sorrow and self-accusation.

Think of the innkeeper. Sometimes someone else has done the rescue, but the healing is a long and complicated process. Can we offer a warm bed, a cool drink of water, or quiet afternoons and evenings to mend broken bodies and hearts? The story doesn't say how long the injured man was at that inn. It doesn't tell us if two silver coins were enough to pay the bill. But I think the innkeeper shared the Samaritan's joy in a way that those who serve always recognize.

I married a Samaritan, a hero. It's true! Ed was a hero, with the medals to prove it. I can't take credit for inspiring him to be a hero, though, since I didn't meet him until after he had won those medals. When Ed was a student at the University of Hawaii, he and many of his friends, also Japanese-American, were members of the ROTC. When the Japanese Imperial Air Force bombed Pearl Harbor and the United States entered World War II, the ROTC and all of the other military units in Hawaii were immediately mobilized as part of the Hawaii Territorial Guard. After enough regular army troops had arrived from the States, Major Frazier, a brawny career officer, called the Japanese-American ROTC cadets into a meeting and, weeping, told them they were being dismissed from the ROTC because their ancestry meant, to those in command, the possibility that they might be disloyal. He was of German ancestry, and he shared with them his own experience of humiliation and frustration during the injustices inflicted upon German-Americans during World War I. He also gave them wonderful advice: "Don't retaliate. Don't fight back. Don't do anything foolish. Don't make it easy for them."

Ed and his friends were heartsick. Ed respected his Japanese ancestors, but he was third-generation Hawaiian and his loyalties were with the United States. He and about three hundred of his friends drafted a petition to the military governor that said, in essence, "Please let us serve our country. If you can't trust us with rifles, let us form labor battalions and replace the city workers who are applying to work for the U.S. Engineers Department. We'll be happy to collect the garbage." These were college students—pre-professionals and well educated. Think of what this request meant to them.

Their request was reluctantly granted, and the VVV (Varsity Victory Volunteers) was formed. They were housed in Schofield Barracks with the soldiers and given the same base pay: $21 a month, from which they had to pay for their own laundry and their own meals. Ed's squad was assigned to a rock-crushing crew. Their job was to run a crushing machine; when rocks were too big to go through the screen, they split them with sledge hammers. A sentry with a rifle and a fixed bayonet guarded them while they did this. Ed and his friends swallowed their humiliation and resentment, made the best of the situation, and soon were best of friends with their guard.

It took a year, but their efforts paid off. The record of the VVVs and the fact that the FBI gave the Japanese-American community of Hawaii a clean bill of health—there wasn't even one documented case of sabotage or disloyalty—meant that the military officials finally took positive action on the repeated petitions of the young Japanese-Hawaiian men to be allowed to serve in the military. A special combat team was formed, the 442nd Infantry, which eventually included 4,500 Japanese-Americans. Its motto was "Go for Broke."

These Japanese-Americans from Hawaii literally competed to get into this unit. Many more applied than there were places for. When the draft quotas were established, the army allotted fifteen hundred places to Hawaiian and three thousand to mainland Japanese-American soldiers. When the recruiting office on the mainland enlisted only five hundred while the recruiting offices in Hawaii were jammed with well-educated young men clamoring to be allowed to enlist, the quotas were reversed. They filled up almost instantly. Some of these young men had fathers and uncles who were interned for the duration of the war because they were prominent businessmen in the Japanese community, or teachers in the Japanese schools, or priests. My uncle was one of them. In our village, Mrs. Yamamoto saw her husband taken to an internment camp while her three sons voluntarily enlisted in the army.

Ed's regimental combat team was sent to Camp Shelby in Hattiesburg, Mississippi, for training. There were about 100,000 men in a town of 30,000 citizens, so things would have been difficult anyway; but conditions were especially hard for the 442nd.

Hattiesburg was a segregated town—this was Mississippi during the 1940s. So there was one door for blacks, and another for whites. But which door should the Japanese use? Where did they fit? The whites definitely didn't want them, but the blacks didn't want them either. Blacks sat at the back of the bus, Caucasians up front; where did the Japanese sit? Ed laughed about trying to find a place to eat, a drinking fountain, a church to attend, even a bathroom to use—but it was hard. The local newspaper ran a hysterical editorial condemning them as spies, there to help the Japanese Imperial Navy invade through the Gulf of Mexico.

Those men had an indomitable spirit. They never lost sight of their goal—to prove their loyalty. When they were sent to

Europe, they were part of the invasion of Italy and fought their way up the peninsula and into France (where Ed was wounded). There are always three regiments in a division. When one regiment attacks, the other two wait in reserve.

The 442nd was a self-contained regiment. It had three battalions of infantry, a company of engineers, one battalion of artillery, and its own medics and anti-tank guns. It wasn't part of a regular division but it could act as a division and was rotated among the different divisions fighting in Italy. It was never held in reserve. Naturally, when the division commander got the 442nd — the way Ed told the story — he would say, "Oh, great! Now I've got some help." So he would attack with one of his three divisions and with the 442nd in the lead. When that section of the line was secured, the division commander would rotate his attack division to the rear to rest while one of the two divisions in reserve came up to the front lines. The 442nd, meanwhile, would be assigned to another division, and the division commander there would say, "Great, now I've got some help!" And he'd attack with one of his divisions and with the 442nd in the lead. So those men were constantly fighting on the front lines. Ed said, "That was good. What we wanted was a chance to prove our loyalty, and that gave us the chance." The 442nd had the highest rate of casualties of any unit fighting in World War II, and it also had the highest rate of decorations. Does that tell the story in a nutshell?

Ed was trained to detect and remove mines in the attack. Whenever the opposing army retreated, it would bury anti-personnel and anti-tank mines in the valleys between the rugged mountains where the traffic would naturally pass. The U.S. army couldn't advance until the mines were out of the way. Ed tells about crawling forward on his hands and knees in the dark, feeling ahead of him for the trigger wires sticking up above the ground. If he felt one, there was a way to jam a pin into the firing mechanism so it wouldn't explode. They would dig up the disarmed mine, and the tanks and infantry could pass. You can imagine what a dangerous job that was and how many men died disarming the mines.

On October 19, 1944, the 442nd was in France. The division they were with was attacking a little hill as part of a larger objective. A regiment of Texans had broken through the German lines but then had been pinned down and surrounded. The 442nd was assigned to rescue them. It was a terrible slaughter. Eight hundred Japanese-Americans died to rescue 341 Texans. (See James Michener, *Hawaii* [New York: Random House, 1959], p. 776.) Ed had been working all night with his squad to clear a mine field. It was raining. He'd slept for just a few minutes, leaning against a tree in his poncho. Just after dawn he got the message that the colonel needed someone to disarm a booby-trapped motorcycle.

Ed thought, "All of my men have worked all night, too. I'll go myself." He was slogging through the rain up the hill with seven other men when the first shell of the morning from the German side, a big 88 mm, came flying over their heads and exploded among them. Three were killed outright. Ed and the other four were wounded, and Ed was awarded the Silver Star. His citation reads as follows: "When Sergeant Okazaki and four other men were wounded by shrapnel . . . he dragged his companions to the safety of a building in the midst of the barrage and, despite his wounds, proceeded to render them first aid. When the aid men arrived and, discovering his bleeding arm, attempted to administer first aid to him he refused medical attention, insisting that he was not seriously wounded. It was not until the four other men had been treated that he consented to receive treatment himself. It was then discovered that he had received three wounds — one in his arm and two in his left leg. Sergeant Okazaki's conspicuous courage, utter disregard for personal safety, and determination were an inspiration to the men of his company."

Ed jokes about his "million-dollar wound," saying it got him out of the war. But it took him a year in the hospital to recover. I often think what a miracle it was that he survived. More than that, it was a miracle that he survived with his gentleness, his kindness, and his good humor intact. That's the man I married.

In Hawaii, people understood and honored his contribution. But during the course of his life he found himself in many other situations where he was judged by his ancestry or for other reasons — usually because he was different in some way from the majority.

What do we do with differences? Do they paralyze us, or can they become part of the beauty of our lives? What are we teaching our children about the beauty of diversity? Are we teaching them that boundaries are barriers, or are we teaching them that a boundary means an opportunity for wonderful explorations in diversity? Emma Lou Thayne interviewed some of her non-LDS friends about living in Utah, and they mentioned the pain experienced by their children as one of the greatest problems:

> [One] finds her children suffering the private grief of being excluded from activities that draw whole neighborhoods of Mormon children together in the warm communion of the ward house. "They could go if they wanted — or I guess if we wanted," I heard, "but not without tying into some realities that we are not prepared to espouse. And without going, they just don't fit."
>
> "Raising Jewish boys," [another] says, "was wonderful until they were twelve or fourteen, when the only friends they knew — all Mormon — started MIA and dropped off somewhere. There was friendliness — but cleavage."

. . . A young mother recalls, "Everything went fine with our four grade schoolers until one day last year. The sixth-grade teacher had all the non-Mormons raise their hands. There were only three. My oldest boy admitted he was Catholic, and from then on he was referred to by the other children as 'dumb Catholic.' Even his best friend has now excluded him — and he feels much more at home at St. Ambrose." ("Ashtrays and Gumwrappers: Women in Utah Mormon Culture," *Task Papers in LDS History, No. 19,* November 1977; typescript in LDS Historical Department, p. 11.)

There's a lot of heartbreak behind these stories. We all know why children behave this way. They want to feel special and important — and Satan's counterfeit way of achieving that goal, even in little children, is to make someone else feel unimportant, unspecial, wrong. Is kindness only for those who are like us? How much like us do they have to be?

When I was teaching elementary school, my principal, Edith Ryberg, was a spunky lady in advance of her time — a truly gifted and inspirational woman. One Monday morning she came to me, shaking her head in disgust. "Chieko, you'll never believe what happened in church yesterday," she said. "The teacher in my Sunday School class said that people who were not born in the covenant hadn't been as valiant in the premortal life as those who were and they wouldn't reach the highest degree of exaltation in the celestial kingdom. I just couldn't stand it. I stood up, told them about you, and said, 'Do you mean to tell me that Chieko Okazaki, who converted herself at the age of fifteen, is not going to be in the highest degree of the celestial kingdom, even if she keeps on being just as righteous for the rest of her life as she has been up to this point?' And the teacher just nodded. I argued and argued, Chieko, but they wouldn't budge."

She told me this with great sorrow, but think of the changes that have been made since then. I can't imagine the same statement being made in a Sunday School class now. In the forty years that have passed, many people who may have believed this way have met good members of the Church from other areas. Their children and grandchildren have served missions all over the world. And we've continued to learn that great lesson of Jesus — that boundaries exist to be crossed.

When people look at other people, what they see on the outside determines what they think. Only when we get close, sit and talk, do we really know the inner heart of the individual. God can see both sides at the same time — the inside and the outside. We can't see both sides at a glance. We have to discover a person's inside, patiently and lovingly. We have to learn to love other people by serving them. How hard is it to see trash blowing toward your neighbor's yard and pick it up? How hard is it to give a neighbor's thirsty child a drink from your hose on a hot day? To wave at them when they drive by? To say, "We have some yellow tulips. I thought they'd look nice with your red tulips, so I brought some over." To learn how to say "Hello" in Tongan, or Samoan, or Spanish? We don't need a formal Church calling to be a source of love and peace, radiating goodwill throughout the neighborhood.

When I think of pure Christianity, I think of Holly and Jean Bach, a Catholic couple who rented our home in Denver for the three years we were on our mission. They let us store our furniture in a downstairs room. They paid the rent exactly on time every month. They never mentioned anything breaking or leaking or needing repairs while we were gone. They were building a home of their own into which they moved a couple of months before we got back, so we expected things to look a little dusty and seedy when we arrived in August 1971. But the house was sparkling clean and in mint condition — exactly as it was when we left. The lawn was freshly mowed, and petunias were blooming in the flower beds. Our neighbors said, "Oh yes, the Bachs planted them this spring so they'd be in bloom when you got back. And Holly came over every week with his push-mower and took care of the lawn." They even paid the rent for the two months they didn't occupy the home. Sometimes we save all of our Christianity for other members of the Church. I'm glad these wonderful Catholic people were so mindful of a Mormon couple. I'd hope we'd all be the same kind of neighbors, no matter what the religion of those who share the neighborhood with us.

Think about your own neighbors. Are they "too" something? Too black, too white, too brown, too red, too clannish, too different, too scary, too Catholic, too Protestant, too liberal, too conservative, too divorced, too many children? The Jews thought the Samaritans were too unrighteous, too racially impure to help them rebuild the temple or to worship with them in it. But I don't think the wounded man lying by the road thought that the wine and oil on his wounds were too Samaritan.

I know that the Lord doesn't think anyone is "too" anything to make a wonderful contribution to the Church. In Africa today, only thirteen years after the revelation granting the priesthood to worthy black men, there are approximately seventeen thousand black Saints. Listen to this wonderful dream told by Jude Inmpey of the Aba area of Nigeria: "He dreamed he was at a major social event where an organ was being played, but the sound from the organ was painful. Upon investigation, he found that the organist was playing only on the white keys. The interpretation came to him sometime later at a Church gathering: 'The Church has for many years played the white keys on the keyboard,' he said, 'and now they're playing both the white and the black, and the music is much sweeter.'"

(E. Dale LeBaron, "Gospel Pioneers in Africa," *Ensign*, August 1990, p. 43.)

In the months since I've been called to my current position, lots of women have asked me, "What's it like to be first counselor in the Relief Society general presidency?" They ask with a little awe. I can tell they're thinking, "Gee, you've really got it made." Usually there's only time to say something quick and general such as, "I just love Relief Society and the sisters. I'm learning so much."

But I think of growing up on a plantation in Mahukona. I think of the Hawaiian women in that tiny Mormon branch who welcomed a Japanese Buddhist girl who edged shyly in the door. They made room for her beside their own children, taught her to sing the hymns, and loved her — not because she was going to be first counselor in the Relief Society general presidency fifty years later, but because she was there and because they had loving hearts.

What do the scriptures say? How do you interpret them? I'm on the path I walk today, because those generous and kind Hawaiian sisters made room for me then.

Nephi left a beautiful reminder and promise: "For [the Lord] inviteth . . . all to come unto him and partake of his goodness; and he denieth none that come unto him, black and white, bond and free, male and female; and he remembereth the heathen; and all are alike unto God, both Jew and Gentile." (2 Nephi 26:33.) May we, too, invite all, deny none.

# CHAPTER TWELVE

# The Power of Charity

CHARITY BEGINS AT HOME. Our families deserve the same kind of thoughtful, sensitive, compassionate service we give our brothers and sisters in need. *We* deserve that kind of charity ourselves.

One problem I saw frequently when working with children was that many were raised in homes with more competition than compassion. It's natural for parents to want their children to achieve, to develop skills in many areas. But some parents get too involved in comparing a child's achievements with those of their other children or of other people's children. Paul describes the antithesis of competitiveness when he says, "Charity suffereth long, and is kind; charity envieth not; charity vaunteth not itself, is not puffed up." (1 Corinthians 13:4.) In contrast, competitiveness is demanding and selfish. It envies the successes of others. It draws attention to its own achievements. And sadly, it considers that personal worth is the same as high achievement.

Now, please don't misunderstand me. Many children are naturally competitive, thrive on a diet of intensive activities, and get their joy from tackling high expectations. You know your children. You know the individual strengths and abilities of each one. What motivates one child to surpass himself or herself may buckle the knees of another child.

Does this mean we should have high standards for some children and low standards for other children? I don't think so. All children need high standards and high expectations. But these standards need to be high in relation to the child's *own* capacity, not in relation to someone else's ability or to some abstract standard of "what all fourth graders should do." What I'm suggesting is that our expectations need to communicate confidence and joy, rather than anxiety and pressure. Sometimes we want our children to do more than they can possibly handle or would choose for themselves. Because we want them to do well in school, because we want them to develop their musical talents, their dramatic abilities, and their athletic gifts, we sometimes unconsciously communicate, "You aren't good enough for me the way you are. I'll like you better when you can do more things or do them better."

Ed and I asked ourselves a question when we talked about goals for our children. Maybe the same question will help you: "If we continue with these same goals and priorities for Ken, will they help him reach his eternal potential?" or "Is our family life right now helping Bob express his eternal nature as a child of God?" Maybe you want to ask other questions: "Is my daughter having opportunities to feel close to her Heavenly Father?" "Is my son having experiences in dealing kindly with others?"

Having a peaceful heart isn't necessarily incompatible with being a great soccer player, but it's not quite clear that having a peaceful heart *depends* on being a great soccer player. If we had to choose between the two of them for our children, what decision would we make?

Many children thrive on busy schedules and seem to be able to switch from one high-intensity activity to another without missing a beat. Other children need more unstructured time to process what's happening to them, to absorb events, and to recharge their batteries before they're ready to come back for more. I'm sure you know the differences among your own children.

When I was a principal, I knew one little second-grader who was always tired. She was a cute little girl, very bright and capable in her schoolwork, but she spent quite a bit of time in the nurse's office. I began to go in and talk to her when I saw her there.

"What makes you so tired?" I asked.

"I have so much to do," she sighed. "I have piano lessons, and ballet lessons, and children's theater to do. And schoolwork, too. It's just too much."

"Do you dislike doing any of those things?" I asked.

"Oh, no. They're all fun and I'm good at all of them," she answered. "But all of them together . . . "

"What do *you* want to do?" I asked.

"Oh," she sighed, "I just wish I had time to *play.*"

I can still see her thin little face, framed by her long brown hair. I talked to her mother. She wasn't a bad mother. She wasn't a psychologically damaged mother who was trying to live her life through her children. She was just trying to give this bright and talented child of hers every opportunity in the world—except the opportunity to be herself and have an unpressured childhood.

I remember another overscheduled child, a little boy. He said, quite matter-of-factly, "I have to take all these classes after school because my mom doesn't want me around too much." Well, I knew his mother. It was obvious that she was not trying to get rid of him, since she was transporting him to all these activities at considerable expense and inconvenience to herself. She just wanted him to explore his talents and enjoy himself, but she was accidentally giving him a different message, one that said, "Having you in these after-school activities is more important than having you with me." Maybe this type of extracurricular involvement had worked with an older sibling, or had worked for her when she was in grade school. But in her effort to give him something *she* thought was important, she was taking away something *he* thought was important: unhurried time and her warm acceptance of who he was just at that moment.

Sometimes children don't know clearly what they want. Sometimes they don't even know clearly what they *don't* want. But often they are surprisingly insightful about their own needs, wants, and circumstances. We teach them respect for their own agency when we give them choices, consult their wishes on optional matters, and let them change their minds when that's possible.

For each child, the balance between keeping busy and happily involved with good things and feeling pressured is probably different. None of them come with instruction manuals, after all! We need to give ourselves permission to do a few experiments and make a few mistakes, too. But one of the great sources of help is our Heavenly Father. Our children are also his children, and he knows things about them that are still hidden from us.

And we are his children too! I wish I could give every anxious mother and every pressured child a certificate that says:

"I hereby bestow upon you the right to have a happy childhood, no matter what age you are. This certificate empowers you to skip through mud puddles, collect snails in a glass jar, stick lilacs in your hair, chase bubbles, tickle a kitten, say hello to the next three people that you meet, act out Mother Goose rhymes, take long bubble baths, get new sneakers, dig holes in the flower bed, give lots of hugs, cry when you're sad, yell when you're mad, tell knock-knock jokes, giggle at puns, talk to Heavenly Father, stay up after midnight and eat ice cream, take apart old clocks, and share snuggles and secrets."

Now, wouldn't that make for a happier childhood? As parents, we want our children to have a happy childhood, and sometimes we need to ease up on them to let that happen. Ask them what they'd like to do and honor as many of those requests as you can. Pay attention to what they enjoy, and see if there's a way to let them have a little bit more of it. Let charity begin at home!

CHARITY FOR YOURSELF

Next, have charity for yourself. I'm giving you permission to have a happy childhood. Right now! It's never too late. As a Relief Society presidency, we receive letters and calls from many wonderful, faithful, righteous LDS women whose lives are burdened and blackened by anxiety, worry, and inappropriate guilt. This guilt is not over sins for which they need to repent, but rather because their expectations of themselves are unrealistically high or because someone who does not understand their life circumstances is making a judgment about them that is painful. Does any of this sound familiar?

We see women who are doing their absolute level best in every way— but they keep track only of their mistakes. They make lists of things they haven't done instead of the phenomenal amount of things they've accomplished. No matter what mountain of achievement they've just climbed, they stumble over molehills, saying things like, "But it's not enough," or, "I didn't do it well enough." Have you given yourself bleak, black messages like these?

The good news of the gospel is that who we are is okay. Our best is good enough. The Savior came for us—just as we are.

Once, after I had spoken in the eastern part of the United States, I received a letter from a woman who, hesitantly and apologetically, asked if it might be possible for her to request a copy of my talk. She wrote, "That was the first meeting I've attended in a long time where I came away with a feeling of self-esteem, rather than thinking, 'Gee, I am really not doing enough.' " Then this wonderful sister explained her circumstances: she had four children, she and her husband were experiencing major financial difficulties, and she then had a time-consuming calling in the Relief Society. Because of infertility problems, her pregnancies were difficult and expensive. Her youngest child was just a few months old, and she felt exhausted, her spirituality drained away, and "suffocated by all the demands." She wanted a calling that was less time-consuming, but the bishop called her to be the Primary president. She wrote me that she felt "awful" about it but "after consulting with my husband, I accepted and trudged forward. . . . I was trying to pull myself out of my 'spiritual slump' but I was not succeeding." Then, just three weeks before the women's conference at which I spoke, she experienced a crisis on Sunday morning before stake conference:

"I was in my kitchen doing breakfast dishes . . . while my family was still eating the breakfast I had prepared. I would not have time to eat and do the dishes and still get ready for church. . . . My mind raced through all the things I was not doing, and I began to shake uncontrollably. I spoke aloud to myself and said, 'I just have to leave.' I hurriedly ran to my bedroom and pulled on jeans and a sweatshirt, grabbed my purse, and went to the car. I had no idea where I would go but I had to leave. I searched through my purse for my car keys. I then realized my husband had used them the night before and they were still in the house. I sat there weeping for a few minutes and further realized that I couldn't leave. I had to be at church in a few minutes. I didn't even have time for a nervous breakdown!"

She went to stake conference, fasting and praying for help, hoping for inspiration. She heard nothing that helped her; it only made her feel worse. The next week, she went to fast meeting but still "felt no better." She wasn't planning to attend the women's meeting at which I spoke because it was held at such a distance from her home; but she found herself there. She concluded, "Much of what I heard at the conference was not new. But this time I truly felt it was from the Lord directed to me. . . . I knew the Lord did hear me, answered me, reassured me, and loves me. I came away fulfilled. My needs were met and I could go on."

Of course, I sent her a copy of the talk. I wish I could have taken it to her personally and sat with her, listened to her story, shared with her my joy that she once again felt that vital connection to the Savior, and maybe gone in with her to share her current circumstances more candidly with her bishop.

Do you know what gives me a tremendous pang in her letter? She had no one to talk to except her husband—no sister in her ward who was there to listen. She doesn't say she even tried to find someone to talk to. In fact, it's as if she didn't *expect* the sisterhood in her area to be any support— this was something she had to do all by herself, and that's why she ended up pouring out her heart to a woman on the other side of the continent whom she'd never met.

There are times when we all come down with terminal Supermom-ism, where we want to do it all and even think we *should* do it all. And I'm concerned. We need to be more supportive of each other. We need to give each other the benefit of the doubt. Peter counseled, "And above all things have fervent charity among yourselves: for charity shall cover the multitude of sins." (1 Peter 4:8.) I like the New International Version of this scripture: "Above all, love each other deeply, because love covers over a multitude of sins." That's good news, isn't it!

Let's stop competing with other women and stop criticizing them, too. Let's stop competing with ourselves and stop picking at ourselves. Let's relax and enjoy who we are. Who we are is enough.

We need to love ourselves. Remember that in a gospel sense *love* means an unconditional desire for the eternal well-being of a soul. Do we feel that we're worthy of such an unconditional regard? Not just someday. Not just if we do everything on the list. But right now?

I love myself. I know I'm imperfect, but I also know that I don't have to judge myself harshly. The Lord is my helper. I can go to him. He loves me and wants an eternity of good things for me. But he also wants to give me seconds, and minutes, and hours of good things right now.

This is true for you, too. He's not waiting for us to become perfect before we can be happy. We can take our time. We can enjoy ourselves. We can consult our own needs and wants. We can forgive ourselves for what we can't do, and we can be patient about the things we can't do yet. We can lighten up and stop punishing ourselves by thinking we have to do it all.

I'll never forget one terrible night, about midnight, when I was frosting a cake for the homemaking luncheon the next day. It wasn't an event I could attend, of course, because I was going to be working. I'd already been working all day—hard. Ed and I had spent the evening with our boys—and there hadn't been much of it left after we had prepared supper, cleaned up, done a few chores, supervised the homework, and talked. That was why I hadn't gotten started on the cake until about ten o'clock, and there I was, exhausted, frosting it. And the next morning, I was going to have to get up early, rush around extra fast, and throw off the schedule for Ed and the boys so that I could squeeze out an extra fifteen minutes to get the cake over to another sister's house before I got myself to work. And at that moment, I had a profound revelation. The revelation was, "This is crazy!"

That revelation gave me enough knowledge and insight so that, the next time a similar situation came up, I could say, "I'm sorry. I just can't right now, but I'd like to another time; or if there's an activity on the weekend, I'd love to help." (I should have discovered sooner that there was a bakery down the street!)

Who we are is all right. God loves us *now!* And what we're doing is an acceptable gift to him. So in addition to having charity for our children, let's save some for ourselves.

CHARITY: THE PURE LOVE OF CHRIST

But what about that commandment to be perfect? If we relax, if we ease off and stop laboring so tensely and intensely, what will happen to our progress toward perfection?

That's a very good question. Let's look at that scripture again, the one that says, "Be ye therefore perfect, even as your Father which is in heaven is perfect." (Matthew 5:48.) What does the Savior mean? What is he talking about in that chapter? Well, for one thing, he's not talking about duties, obedience, and responsibilities. This is the Sermon on the Mount, and he's talking about being blessed, letting our lights shine, avoiding anger and quarreling, going the second mile, and—now we're getting to the section that this verse belongs to—about loving our neighbors but also loving our enemies. He talks about his Father who, in a parched desert land, sends rain "on the just and on the unjust" and permits his sun "to rise on the evil and on the good." *Then* he says, "Be ye therefore perfect, even as your Father . . . is perfect."

How is our Father perfect? In not withholding the blessings of his sun and rain—which I think are symbols for his love—from anyone. I think the Savior is trying to tell us in the Sermon on the Mount that love doesn't make distinctions about whether someone is evil or good, deserving or not deserving. Love will spill over in blessing, simply because that's the nature of love.

That's the kind of love we should aspire to — the same kind of love that the Father has. "And above all these things," writes Paul, "put on charity, which is the bond of perfectness. And let the peace of God rule in your hearts, to the which also ye are called in one body; and be ye thankful." (Colossians 3:14–15.)

Our Heavenly Father has gone through this learning process himself. He has a profound understanding of what we have to do. He has a goal for us. He wants us to all return to him, but he nowhere says that we all have to be the same to do that. If we set out on our journey back to him, dragging ourselves along out of duty, feeling pounded and pounced on and harried by our righteous desires, what will we have to give God at the end of that road?

I think God's timetable for us is probably different from the expectations we have for ourselves. We only imperfectly grasp his immense patience. When Ed and I were serving our mission in Japan, Elder and Sister Bruce R. McConkie came to tour the mission. One of the places within our mission boundaries that they wanted to see was the Noritake china factory, so we visited it with them. We had a wonderful tour and saw many beautiful things, but the most impressive thing to me was the reject barrels. At every stage of the process, standing next to the conveyor belts that carried the dishes along, were large barrels. When the dishes were formed out of the clay, someone looked at each cup, each saucer, each plate. If there was a flaw in it, crash! It went flying into the barrel. After it had been fired in the kiln, there would be another inspection. Again, if there was a flaw, crash! Then the glaze was applied and inspected. Crash!

Crash! And then the pattern was painted on. There was another inspection. There were more crashes.

At that point, I became worried. There seemed to be so much waste. Did the inspectors really need to be this rigorous? I mentioned these barrels to our guide. He laughed and said, "You mustn't worry. Nothing is ever wasted. All of the items in the barrels are taken back to the beginning, reground, reshaped, and started on their journey again. But it must be perfect to be Noritake."

This experience was illuminating to me as I thought about the need we have to achieve perfection. There is no waste. And there is no haste. We will all have all the time we need. We have a loving Father who makes sure we will receive the experiences we need to achieve perfection. He will let us start over again as often as we need to.

There's one part of the example I don't want you to misunderstand. I don't think we need to be inspectors. I don't think we need to inspect ourselves. Life is inspecting us. And we definitely don't need to inspect other people. That's like a cup inspecting a saucer. We can leave that part to our Heavenly Father.

## CHARITY FOR OTHERS

What does charity mean when it's applied to compassionate service? I think sometimes we read these beautiful scriptures and think, "Charity is really something incredible. We have to be like Jesus—willing to be crucified. It's mysterious. It's mystical. It's something that's too hard (or too big, or too complicated) for me to do."

I have a very simple, uncomplicated view of charity. It's ordinary kindness. It's common courtesy. It's everyday thoughtfulness. It's simple sensitivity. It's the Golden Rule. It's putting yourself in the place of the other person and saying,

"How would I like to be treated?" I think that 99 percent of our difficulties with the concept of charity would disappear altogether if we just kept this view in mind.

I was in a committee meeting on sesquicentennial projects when the subject of having a charitable perspective came up. Three of the women there told unbelievable stories about insensitivity. The first woman had a relative who was elderly, widowed, and crippled with arthritis. During one severe winter when this elderly sister hadn't been out of the house for days, the bishopric visited her little home. The snow on her front sidewalk was so deep that they were soaked to the knees by the time they got to her door. She welcomed them in, and as they sat in her living room, the bishop asked, "Well, Sister So-and-so, is there anything we can do for you?" She didn't say what she was thinking: "Bishop, what did you just wade through to get into my house? Does that give you a clue?"

The second story came from a single sister who found her backyard so overgrown with weeds that they were up to her knees. She was hacking away at them with a dull hoe, feeling sweaty, breathless, and outnumbered, when her home teachers came by. One was a husky teenager and the other was a healthy, middle-aged man. They leaned over her fence and called, "Well, hello, Sister So-and-so. Looks like you're busy. We'll come back another time." She said, "I was speechless. And I was so mad, it's a good thing that I *couldn't* say anything!"

The third woman said her sister was lying in bed, too sick to get up, when the visiting teachers rang the doorbell. The three-year-old answered the door, and the woman heard this conversation from her bedroom:

"Where's your mommy, honey? Isn't she home with you?"

"Oh, yes," said the three-year-old, "but she's sick in bed."

"Oh, that's too bad," said the visiting teacher. "Tell her we stopped by and we'll come back when she's feeling better."

I was flabbergasted. How could things like this happen in a church where we've had 150 years of "charity never faileth"? It sounded to me as if charity never faileth because it's never been tried! It doesn't require moral sophistication to put yourself in the position of another person and think what needs to be done.

Ed is a terrific home teacher; and I found out recently that he's a pretty terrific visiting teacher, too. In February 1991 when I was in New Zealand, one of the sisters I visit teach lost her unborn baby. When I got back from my trip, I visited her. The first thing she said was, "Do you know what Ed did?"

Ed hadn't told me anything except that she'd lost her baby. But as soon as she had come home from the hospital, Ed was there with some flowers and a card. He said, "Chieko is in New Zealand, and I know she would have brought food for you and offered to help. I'm not so sure you'd like the way I cook, but I want to bring you some comfort." She said, "And then he telephoned me every couple of days to make sure I was all right. He's the kindest man."

And then I found out something else he'd done while I was on that same trip. A friend from Denver had left a message on the recorder asking how things were going. Ed sent her back a note saying, "If Chieko were here, she would have answered your call; but she's in New Zealand on an assignment. I just wanted you to know she's not neglecting you." Ed didn't tell me about this act of kindness, either; again, I learned about it from my friend. This is charity—seeing a need and filling it with love.

The reason "charity never faileth" is because we aren't in charge of the supply department. Love comes from our Heavenly Father and Jesus Christ, spilling over into our own hearts until we simply brim over with love into the lives of others. Amy Brown Lyman, the sixth general president of the Relief

Society, said, "Charity does more than give to the needy—it sympathizes with those in distress, comforts those who mourn, forgives those who do wrong; charity seeks to build up rather than to tear down character; it refrains from unkind or unfair criticism. It helps those who are weak to rise and then assists in sustaining them."

Let's remember that charity begins at home. Let's focus on loving our children for who they are right now and eliminating the feeling for them that they have to compete and struggle and achieve to be good enough. Let's focus on loving ourselves for who we are right now. We don't need to compete with an image of impossible perfection. Let's focus on letting love flow to our sisters and brothers. Let's accept and rejoice in their diversity. Let's offer the gift of understanding and acceptance. We don't need to judge. We don't need to compare. There's room for all of us. Let's allow our love for Jesus to take the form of simple kindness and courtesy whenever we see a need.

Truly, "now we see through a glass, darkly; but then face to face: now I know in part; but then shall I know even as also I am known. And now abideth faith, hope, charity, these three; but the greatest of these is charity." (1 Corinthians 13:12–13.)

# CHAPTER THIRTEEN

# "Neither Do I Condemn Thee..."

WHEN THE SCRIBES AND PHARISEES brought to Jesus the woman taken in adultery, attempting to trap him, he turned the trap back on them with the words, "He that is without sin among you, let him first cast a stone at her." And hearing this, they were "convicted by their own conscience" and quietly slipped away until "Jesus was left alone, and the woman standing in the midst. When Jesus had lifted up himself [from writing on the earth], and saw none but the woman, he said unto her, Woman, where are those thine accusers? hath no man condemned thee? She said, No man, Lord. And Jesus said unto her, Neither do I condemn thee: go, and sin no more." (John 8:2–11.)

Think of the balm he poured on that woman's bruised spirit! She was guilty as charged, and he acknowledged that by telling her to leave her sins behind her. But he told her to go as a free woman into that new life. He did not make her acknowledge her guilt. He did not humiliate her. He did not rub her nose in it. Think of the empowerment with which she stepped forward into that new life!

This story about Jesus and the adulterous woman teaches us about self-esteem based on having a personal, firsthand understanding of the Savior and his charity, or pure love. Today we are barraged by accusing voices. People seem to stand in line to condemn us. And if the line gets short, we stand in it ourselves to make ourselves feel guilty. We feel guilty for things we have done, for things we haven't done, for things we did but did wrong, for doing too much, for doing too little, for doing things at the wrong time, for doing things at the wrong place, for wearing the wrong color of shoes when we did them—you name it! We're guilty!

What is the message of the gospel? Is it that we're weak, frail sinners? That Heavenly Father is disgusted and angry with us? That Jesus is sorry he died for us because it was a real waste of the Atonement? That all the angels have decided that giving us agency was a stupid thing to do? No! The message of the scriptures is that *nothing* can separate us from the love of Christ. Paul, in trying to make his Roman converts understand this, wrote this beautiful, powerful passage: "If God is for us, who can be against us? He who did not spare his own Son, but gave him up for us all—how will he not also, along with him, graciously give us all things? Who will bring any charge against those whom God has chosen? . . . Who is he that condemns? Christ Jesus, who died—more than that, who was raised to life—is at the right hand of God . . . interceding for us. Who shall separate us from the love of Christ? Shall trouble or hardship or persecution or famine or nakedness or danger or sword? . . . No, in all these things we are more than conquerors through him who loved us. For I am convinced that neither death nor life, neither angels nor demons, neither the present nor the future, nor any powers, neither height nor depth, nor anything else in all creation, will be able to separate us from the love of God that is in Christ Jesus our Lord." (NIV, Romans 8:31–39.)

Isn't that thrilling! Doesn't this knowledge sweep away all those sneering, accusing faces? Doesn't that affirmation of love roar like a mighty wind in your ears, drowning out those scoffing, accusing voices? Paul affirms: "For we do not have a high priest who is unable to sympathize with our weaknesses, but we have one who has been tempted in every way, just as we are — yet was without sin. Let us then approach the throne of grace with confidence, so that we may receive mercy and find grace to help us in our time of need." (NIV, Hebrews 4:15 16.)

Don't you feel your courage rise at the thought of coming boldly to the throne of grace, knowing we will find arms outstretched in welcome and never-failing love?

The Apostle John told his converts this: "And if any man [or woman] sin, we have an *advocate* with the Father, Jesus Christ the righteous." (1 John 2:1; emphasis added.) He doesn't turn away from us when we sin; he cherishes us, takes our side, argues for us.

And it's not just a matter of finding a welcome when we come to Jesus. No, he's not waiting for us, hoping we'll drop in. He is actively seeking us. He is the good shepherd, out walking through the night, calling the name of the lost sheep. He is the good housewife, lighting a candle and sweeping in dark corners to find the lost coin. He has come to our door, and there he stands, knocking, hoping we will hear and open the door and welcome him in. And what rejoicing there is when the sheep lifts its head and bleats, and the shepherd comes scrambling over the rocks! With what joy the housewife catches the first gleam of the lost coin and stretches out her hand to pick it up! What jubilation when the door hinges creak and the door begins to open, just a crack! Keep listening to that voice. "Neither do I condemn thee. Neither do I condemn thee!"

This is the good news of the gospel! Where do those other voices come from, those scribe voices, those Pharisee voices? Why do they have such power to shame us? Why do they make us wander away from the fold, hide in dark corners, slam the

157

door shut against the divine visitor who stands and knocks? They come from Satan. And Satan is the father of lies.

"Oh no," you say, "it's not a lie. It's true that I'm a bad person. I skip church. I get mad at my kids. I'm too fat. I don't pray every day. I wish my neighbors would drop dead. I can't stop smoking. I watch soap operas." But remember Jesus and the woman. He didn't say, "You really are a disgusting woman. You really did commit adultery." He said, "Neither do I condemn thee."

Though it was true that she had done something wrong, he affirmed her *self*, her very being. He created a relationship of acceptance with her, instead of one that condemned her. How do you think she felt?

Think back to something that is a painful part of your life, something that has caused you grief and shame. It could be something that's happened recently or something that happened a long time ago. It could be something only you know about, or it could be something many people know about. It just has to be something that is associated with feelings of shame or embarrassment and pain for you. Bring that painful thing, whatever it is, before your eyes so that you're looking it right in the face, so that you acknowledge that it happened, so that you see it and feel it. Now, turn this painful companion around so that the two of you are standing side by side. Picture a man in a rough, homespun robe, stooped over writing something on the ground with his finger. He straightens up and looks at you — at both of you together — and he says, "Neither do I condemn thee." Hear those words in your mind and say them to yourself in your heart: "Neither do I condemn thee. Come follow me."

As you say those words, the companion of pain and embarrassment and torment beside you leaves — just turns around and walks away — and you watch it go. You don't call it back.

You don't chase after it. You don't ask, "Where are you going?" You just watch it until it is out of sight. It's getting farther and farther away. And now it's gone. And then you realize that Jesus is standing next to you. He's your new companion. He looks into your eyes, smiles, and asks, as if it's a private little joke between the two of you, "Now where's that accuser? Who's condemning you?" and you say, "No one, Lord."

You know what left your life just now. Remember, it's gone. You have a new companion. You have a friend beside you who is an advocate, not an accuser. You have someone with you who will *never* condemn you. Believe it! What you have just done is to accept the atonement of the Savior.

We hear a lot about self-esteem these days. Self-esteem — the kind that really counts — comes from a relationship with Jesus Christ and Heavenly Father that is real and solid and alive. Not a secondhand relationship of listening to someone else talk about them, but a firsthand relationship of talking with them, of experiencing their love, of being their hands in serving others.

The first focus point of our Relief Society program is to "build personal testimony." Elaine Jack explained this as "leading lives of faith and hope, and becoming thoughtful, prayerful disciples of our Savior." ("These Things Are Manifested Unto Us Plainly," *Ensign,* November 1990, p. 90.)

Much guilt and anger and low self-esteem come when we get wrongful messages about who we are — from people who don't know us but who judge us, from people who restrict us from being who we are. Remember that Jesus sees us as we are and knows us to the very foundation of our being and loves us enough that he died for us — more than that, as Paul reminds us — came alive again for us.

Now, if Jesus knows us so well — so much better than we can ever know another person in the limits of mortality — and he still loves us, we are relieved from the terrible burden of having to decide who is worthy to love and who isn't. We don't need to judge. And we don't need to be judged. Don't judge other people and don't let other people judge you.

"How do I do that?" you ask. "Don't I have to decide whether something is good or bad before I can choose it?" Some*thing*, yes. Some*one*, no. We really don't have to spend a lot of time thinking about whether something is good or bad. Most of us can tell the difference easily.

You know how you take a mouthful of good wheat bread and chew it slowly, savoring the texture and the taste and the right flavor of it? By the time you've swallowed it, you could tell someone else quite a bit about that mouthful of bread. You could tell whether it was sweetened with honey or molasses or sugar. You could say whether it had enough salt or too much or too little for your taste. You could talk about whether the crust was chewy or crispy.

Then suppose you take a mouthful of moldy bread by mistake. Do you have to chew it and roll it around in your mouth and think about it to know that it's bad? No. You just spit it out and brush your teeth. Maybe you can't use as many adjectives or talk as long about the moldy bread as you could about the good bread, but you don't have to. All you have to do is identify it as bad and get rid of it. Can you think of something in your life that you need to just spit out? Well, do it, and then go brush your teeth and get on with making a new batch of bread.

In dealing with each other, the moral of this story is that you don't need to spend a lot of time pointing out to other people what they are doing wrong. You don't have to make them admit that they are doing wrong and force them to grovel over it. You don't have to rub their noses in their mistakes. Just help them free themselves and step forward into change with as little hindrance as possible. This is a principle that works with everybody.

For example, when I was an elementary school principal, one of my teachers sent a boy to the office. His family had moved into the area recently from another state, and it was a family that communicated with a lot of swear words. This boy used that language regularly, and the teacher couldn't deal with it so she sent him to the office. I read the note and looked at the boy and just laughed. I said, "Isn't it wonderful that you speak two languages!"

That was probably the last thing he was expecting. He looked at me and said, "I don't speak two languages."

"Oh yes," I said. "You speak English and you speak another language, too, one that your teacher has been trying to work with you on. Isn't that true?"

His eyes dropped and he said sullenly, "I suppose so." I didn't want him to feel defensive so I said, "Well, you know, some of us don't understand that language very well, but in school we all understand English. Would you mind just using the English language at school? You can use your other language at home—that's fine—but here, could you try using school language?"

He said, "I guess so."

"I know it will be hard," I continued. "But especially when you get angry, try hard to think of something else you could say, something that's in the English language—like 'Don't do that' or 'Oh, shucks.' Do you think you can do that?"

"Yeah," he said. "I'll bet I can." And he was smiling. It *was* hard for him, but he tried. And whenever I saw him in school, I'd give him a big hug and say, "And how's the English language coming?" And he'd laugh and say, "I'm working on it."

What would have happened if I had condemned that boy, told him he was doing wrong, told him his parents were wrong for using that kind of language at home? He would have defended his parents, defended himself, and defied both me and his teacher. But this was a way to let him change that didn't burden him as he tried to make that change.

It takes a lot of courage and a long time to change. If you are a convert, you understand what I'm saying. Give yourself credit for the changes that you've made and don't pick on yourself for the changes that you haven't made yet. When we compare our old ways with our new aspirations, our self-esteem goes down. When we compare the new with the ideal, our self-esteem goes *way* down. Remember the Savior's way: "Neither do I condemn thee."

Not long ago I received a wonderful letter from a dear friend I'd known in Denver, Lynnanne Eddington. She wrote:

"About seven years ago, I pondered the question, 'If the road is so strait and narrow, then how come we all do these different things?' [From my perspective now,] the road seems pretty wide to me. This past week I substituted in early morning seminary, and also for the sixteen- and seventeen-year-olds in Sunday School. It was great! I relearned some things. The path is strait and narrow; however, each person's stepping stones are not necessarily in the same order. And like you once said, it's not where we are but where we are going that matters, and we ought to be lending a helping hand to each other as we walk the path.

"Perhaps instead of criticizing one another for whatever, we might bear testimony of those steps we know to be needful and helpful. There is not just one way to hold family home evening or study the scriptures or learn to read or gain a testimony, although at some point we must put Moroni's promise to the test. I love idea sharing. As I share ideas with friends,

I receive wonderful ideas that I can adapt to fit the needs of my own family."

I love that letter because it captures the spirit of two of our five focus points in Relief Society: "Bless the individual woman" (and that means all of the wide diversity of women in Relief Society) and "Develop and exercise charity." As a Relief Society presidency, we chose these goals because we want them to be positive, affirming aspects of life for Mormon women. But they can either build or decrease self-esteem, depending on whether you give yourself credit for the good things you've done or blame yourself for not quite measuring up to your goals.

Another of our Relief Society focus points is to strengthen families. That means that during the season of family building, it's your top job. Work and Church service come lower on the list. I see women who are working as hard as they can. Their jobs, their Church work, and their families are a merry-go-round that keeps spinning faster and faster for them. They know they can't do it all but they feel they must. They drive themselves harder than they can go, and then punish themselves for failing. What happens to your self-esteem when you get trapped in a situation like this?

Well, know yourself. Know the season you're in. Know when to say no. Your first responsibility is to your husband and children. If you're a single mother, you have a double responsibility to your children. Know what you can and what you can't do.

What do you do when you're called to a Church responsibility? Do you feel that you must say yes, no matter what? I think it's important to serve, but a ward needs lots of workers and has lots of different tasks. You know what it takes to staff a ward. Look at that long list of jobs and think which one you could realistically do. Ask for an interview with the bishop and explain your situation to him. Maybe this isn't your season to be an executive in an auxiliary or even a teacher who has weekly responsibilities. You shouldn't tell the bishop how to do his calling, but share your life stage and circumstances with him. If you can serve in a calling, you should do it, do it with all your might, and rejoice in it. It will be a blessing to you, and your self-esteem will increase. But if you say yes to a calling you really can't manage, then you feel guilty. It tears you down and drags you down. Be wise in what you say yes to.

Furthermore, negotiate! It doesn't always have to be "yes" or "no." When we were living in Denver, Ed looked at the program for the young men and saw that the Scouting program just wasn't very good—and we had two boys who were Scouts. He went to the bishop, explained what he saw, explained his own circumstances and abilities, and said, "I'm not telling you what to do, but I'd be willing to serve as Scoutmaster." He was called to be Scoutmaster almost overnight! And he stayed Scoutmaster until our boys and dozens of others had their Eagles. He made himself available for a calling that he wanted to do. You can do the same thing.

Recently I negotiated with my Relief Society president over my visiting teaching calling. My companion traveled a lot, as I did, and it was difficult for us to get together. We had four sisters to visit: two who came to everything, and two with whom I'd developed a special relationship, but who wouldn't let anybody else in. I wanted to keep visiting those two women, and I had to do it without a companion because they wouldn't allow anyone else to visit them. The circumstances were such that the Relief Society president saw my point. You can discuss things like that, too.

I think of a wonderful Hawaiian woman I know, Winifred Watanabe Chinen. Her husband is not a member of the Church and has poor health. He allows her to attend meetings but refuses to allow her to accept any callings. Knowing his feelings, the bishop has not asked Sister Chinen to accept any callings. It certainly would be possible for her to feel downcast and discouraged by her situation, but instead, this is what she says: "I've decided that I do not need any calling. I volunteer for whatever I can do, in whatever capacity I can be of use in our Relief Society to relieve the president of any mundane responsibilities." She cares for the sacrament cloths, brings flowers for the chapel, does visiting teaching, and renders compassionate service. "Being there and helping" at any Relief Society function is her calling. Her very countenance radiates a "brightness of hope." Instead of dwelling on the things she cannot do, she focuses on what she can do, attends her meetings with real gratitude, and constantly seeks out others in her neighborhood to help. I would wager that she does as much good as any so-called fully active Latter-day Saint in Hawaii.

What if we could see ourselves as the Lord sees us? What if we knew our strengths and talents as clearly as he does? Sometimes we think, "I'm just the same old me. Nothing has changed. I've always been this way and I'll always be this way." Not so! Heavenly Father knows the full range of our potential and powers and has sent the Holy Ghost to dwell in us. "As Christ was raised up from the dead by the glory of the Father, even so we also should walk in newness of life." (Romans 6:4.)

Let us walk forward into that newness of life. We can do it, for beside us is a loving, living companion who will not condemn us!

# Seeking the Light of Christ

# CHAPTER FOURTEEN

# Opening the Door to Christ

LET'S CONSIDER THE SIGNIFICANCE of the invitation the Savior offered us, as recorded in John: "I am the door: by me if any man enter in, he shall be saved, and shall go in and out, and find pasture. . . . I am come that they might have life, and that they might have it more abundantly." (John 10:9–10.)

While on the isle of Patmos, John returned to this image of Christ as the door, when he wrote this stirring revelation of things to come: "These things saith he that is holy [and by this, John means the Savior], he that is true, he that hath the key of David, he that openeth, and no man shutteth; and shutteth, and no man openeth; I know thy works." (Revelation 3:7–8.)

Usually when someone says, "I know your works. I know what you're doing," don't we usually think, "Oh, no! You know what I'm *doing!*" and begin to feel guilty or self-conscious! There's a tendency to assume we're doing something wrong, isn't there? Yet in this instance, there's not a shadow of accusation or blame or guilt in the words of Jesus. He is speaking in comfort, in promise, in assurance, in might: "I know thy works: behold, I have set before thee an open door, and no man can shut it: for thou hast a little strength, and hast kept my word, and hast not denied my name." (V. 8.) Isn't there a feeling of triumph in what he's saying? He sets before us an open door that we are completely free to walk in and out of, as we choose. No one can close that door between us and the Savior. In fact, he himself is that door. We have total, complete access.

If we want to "come unto Christ," as Moroni says, "and be perfected in him, and deny [ourselves] of all ungodliness; . . . and love God with all [our] might, mind and strength," the door is open. Nothing can hinder us. Nothing can make us stumble. No one can bar the way. No one can keep us out. Instead, the promise is that "then is his grace sufficient for you, that by his grace ye may be perfect in Christ." (Moroni 10:32.) Notice that it doesn't say we'll be perfect in ourselves. It says we'll be "perfect in Christ."

Going back to that same chapter of Revelation we saw earlier, we read one more thing that Jesus says about the door: "Behold, I stand at the door, and knock: if any man hear my voice, and open the door, I will come in to him, and will sup with him, and he with me." (Revelation 3:20.)

That's a little different, isn't it? It says, "I stand at the door and knock." It doesn't say, "Here I come, ready or not." It doesn't say, "Okay, you have an appointment with me from 10:15 to 10:25 A.M. on Wednesday." It says that Christ stands, knocking and waiting. Waiting for us to hear his voice and open the door.

Isn't that a breathtaking idea? If we want to go to Christ, the door is open and nothing can bar our way. But if Christ wants to come to us, he comes to the door. He stands patiently on the doorstep, knocking, hoping that we will hear him calling, hoping that we will open the door. The door to him is always open. But the door to *us* is not open. We have to choose to open it.

What keeps that door closed? A lot of things do. Sometimes we feel ashamed that we aren't already perfect; we don't understand that we can't be perfect unless it's in Christ. I think we're distracted sometimes by the things of this world. At times we lack love and faith. There are occasions when our hearts are divided. But it's our broken, divided, hurting hearts that he wants. He begs us to offer him "a broken heart and a contrite spirit" (2 Nephi 2:7) so that he can make his atoning sacrifice operational in our behalf. It is the broken heart that must be offered to Jesus Christ, and it is the humble heart that he can heal.

We live in a world that breaks our hearts, that fragments us, that pulls different pieces of us away so that we end up with huge chunks missing. And we give pieces of our hearts away — to making money, to having a bigger house, to struggling in a relationship that doesn't work, to worrying about the future, to being depressed about the past. It's easy to see that these things are negative. They don't enhance our relationship with the Savior — in fact, they hinder it — and they don't make us better people.

But we also break our hearts over positive things — over our children, over our callings. We worry about a child going astray, and our heart goes with him. We know that another child is having trouble finding work, and part of our heart is fixed on her. Maybe we don't want a bigger house, but we want a cleaner house, and part of our heart hangs there. We give parts of our hearts to our jobs, to our bosses, to the family home evening manual. We're grateful when the bishop tells us we're doing a good job teaching the Young Women. We melt in tears when we hear a Mother's Day speaker talk about the joys of motherhood. And our hearts keep fragmenting and fragmenting.

Are you feeling confused at this point? "Wait a minute," you're saying to yourself. "Aren't these good things? Aren't we supposed to value and want them?"

Yes, we are. But first, and above all else, we are supposed to desire the Lord. In Japan, there is an ancient ascetic tradition.

A significant number of people who feel drawn toward the spiritual life leave their daily pursuits and enter monasteries where they fast, meditate, and train their minds and spirits to abandon this world and experience bliss. Other Christian religions also have a similar tradition. Those who feel drawn toward the spiritual life have ways of withdrawing from the world, and it is accounted as righteousness to them.

There is no ascetic or cloistered tradition in Mormonism. The gospel calls us, not to the next world or to another world, but to this world. Our temples are the ultimate retreats from the world, but the celestial room is a place to reach and linger only for a few moments. It's not a place where we can take up residence. We're invited and counseled to come to the temple often, but nobody has ever told us we should try to stay there.

There's a simple reason for that. The gospel is not a system that distrusts or despises the world. We love the earth our Heavenly Father created for us. This is the world Jesus Christ was born in as a baby, a baby who had to learn how to eat, sit up, walk, and talk.

The commandment to work is imposed on us by our descent from Adam and Eve, but it is a blessing to us. Illness and adversity are not punishments for being alive; they are natural accompaniments of life. Our bodies are not vile and loathsome snares for our spirits, but the temples of our spirits. The daily activities of mixing orange juice, making telephone calls, supervising homework, and scrubbing the bathtub are not distractions from our spiritual lives. They are the vehicles through which we live our spiritual lives.

The Savior does not call us to abandon the world; he calls us to come unto him so that he can heal us and make us whole. But to do that, we have to bring him our hearts — all of the pieces we have given elsewhere. We have to care about him more than we care about the orange juice, the telephone, the homework, the dirty bathtub. He asks us to take care of our daily activities with a heart centered on him. With whole hearts we can worship him through all those quite ordinary activities of our mortality.

I think we sometimes have the mistaken notion that religion is like a special room in our house. We go into this room when we need to "do" religion. After all, we cook in the kitchen, we entertain in the living room, we wash in the bathroom, we sleep in the bedroom, and we "do" religion in this spiritual room. The fallacy of this view of religious life is obvious. It means that we can walk out of that room and close the door behind us. It means that we have compartmentalized our lives so that religious experience is just one cubbyhole out of many. It also means that we spend most of our time in other rooms. Yet we feel guilty because we're taught repeatedly that this should be the most important room in the house and we should spend most of our time there. Does this sound even a tiny bit familiar?

Rather than think of spiritual life as a separate room, let's think of it as paint on the walls of all the rooms, or maybe a scent in the air that drifts through the whole house—the way the fragrance of spaghetti sauce or baking bread has a way of drifting through all the rooms of the house, becoming part of the air we breathe. Our spiritual lives should *be* our lives, not just a separate part of our lives.

Suppose the Savior were to come to visit you. You've rushed around and vacuumed the guest room, put the best sheets on the bed, even placed some tulips in a vase on the dresser. Jesus looks around the room and says, "Oh, thank you for inviting me into your home. Please tell me about your life."

You say, "I will in just a minute, but something's boiling over on the stove, and I also need to let the cat outside."

173

Jesus says, "I know a lot about cats and stoves. I'll come with you."

"Oh, no," you say. "I couldn't let you do that." And you rush out, carefully closing the door behind you.

While you're turning down the stove, the phone rings, and then Jason comes in with a scrape on his elbow, and the visiting teaching supervisor calls for your report, and then it's supper-time, and you couldn't possibly have Jesus see that you don't even have placemats on the table, and someone forgot to turn on the dishwasher so you're eating off paper plates, and then you have to drive Lynne to her basketball game. By the time you get back to the room where Jesus is waiting patiently, you're so tired that you can barely keep your eyes open, let alone sit worshipfully at his feet waiting for words of profound wisdom and spiritual power to wash over you, to make you different, to make everything else different, and you fall asleep whispering, "I'm sorry. I'll try to do better. I'm so sorry."

How we pour guilt over ourselves!

This isn't the gospel. We know that on some level Jesus experienced the totality of mortal existence in Gethsemane. It's our faith that he experienced everything—absolutely everything. Sometimes we don't think through the implications of that belief. We talk in great generalities about the sins of all humankind, about the suffering of the entire human family. But we don't experience pain in generalities. We experience it individually. That means Jesus knows what it felt like when your mother died of cancer—how it was for your mother, how it still is for you. He knows what it felt like to lose the student-body election. He knows that moment when the brakes locked, and the car started to skid. He experienced the slave ship sailing from Ghana toward Virginia. He experienced the gas chambers at Dachau. He experienced napalm in Vietnam. He knows about drug addiction and alcoholism.

There is nothing you have experienced *as a woman* that he does not also know and recognize. On a profound level, he understands about pregnancy and giving birth. He knows about PMS and cramps and menopause. He understands about rape and infertility and abortion.

His last recorded words to his disciples were, "And, lo, I am with you alway, even unto the end of the world." (Matthew 28:20.) What does that mean? It means he understands your mother-pain when your five-year-old leaves for kindergarten, when a bully picks on your fifth-grader, when your daughter calls to say that the new baby has Down's syndrome. He knows your mother-rage when a trusted babysitter sexually abuses your two-year-old, when someone gives your thirteen-year-old drugs, when someone seduces your seventeen-year-old. He knows the pain you live with when you come home to a quiet apartment where the only children who ever come are visitors, when you hear that your former husband and his new wife were sealed in the temple last week, when your fiftieth wedding anniversary rolls around and your husband has been dead for two years. He knows all that. He's been there. He's been lower than all that.

So do you really think you're shielding him by keeping the door closed while you're throwing paper plates on the table and sending Chrissie off to wash her hands for the second time? Do you really think he doesn't know? doesn't understand? wouldn't laugh and help?

But he'll stay in that room if you put him there. The door to him is always open, but the door to you can be closed and stay closed — if you choose to close it. If one great constant in the universe is the unfailing love of the Savior, the other great constant is his unfailing respect for human agency. He will not override your will, even for your own good. He will not compel you to accept his help. He will not force you to accept his companionship. He leaves you free to choose.

I beg you to open the door and let him out of that room. Give him your whole heart, all the pieces, and let him heal you. He promises, "And ye shall seek me, and find me, when ye shall search for me with all your heart." (Jeremiah 29:13.) *With all our hearts.* That means we don't have pieces of our hearts that he doesn't touch or that aren't relevant to him. That means we must live our lives as Savior-focused individuals. Jesus doesn't call you to abandon Jason's scraped elbow when you come unto him. He calls you to bandage Jason's scraped elbow as a Savior-focused mother. Let him be with you as you bandage Jason's scrape. Let him join in the conversation over those soggy paper plates. Let him carpool with you, fill out the quarterly budget with you, attend that sales seminar with you, talk over that Young Women's lesson with your daughter, try out for the wrestling team with your son, be with your mother when the doctor tells her the diagnosis.

He's not waiting for us to be perfect. Perfect people don't need a Savior. He came to save us in our imperfections. He is the Lord of the living, and the living make mistakes. He's not embarrassed by us, angry at us, or shocked. He wants us in our brokenness, in our unhappiness, in our guilt and our grief.

You know that people who live above a certain latitude and experience long winter nights can become depressed and even suicidal, because something in our bodies requires whole-spectrum light for a certain number of hours a day. Our spiritual requirement for light is just as desperate and as deep as our physical need for light. Jesus is the light of the world. We know that this world is a dark place sometimes, but we need not walk in darkness. The people who sit in darkness have seen a great light, and the people who walk in darkness can have a bright companion. We need him, and he is ready to come to us, if we'll open the door and let him.

Now, let's get down to the realities of our lives. We have an imperfect world with built-in adversities. We have a world in which everyone is different. There's an incredible amount of diversity in our backgrounds, in our spiritual gifts, in our desires, in our experiences, in our educational levels, in our Church experience. And we each have agency. Our Heavenly Father knew that these facts would cause trouble and sin, but he also knew that it was the only way to get true faith, true goodness, and even godhood. So here we are. How shall we live our lives? And how can we make Jesus part of our lives instead of leaving him in the guest room?

Let's review a couple of the conditions that make mortality what it is. Because of our human limitations on time and ability, we must make choices—and we will sometimes make mistakes. We don't have the answers just handed to us. Instead, we must think, work, and maybe try a few alternatives. Prayer is our lifeline in this process of staying close to the Savior.

## THE RESPONSIBILITY OF CHOICE

Do you ever have the feeling that you have more things you'd like to do than you really *can* do in a day? More things you *need* to do than will fit in a day? Guess what? You're probably not alone. Let's just take a couple of responsibilities you might have. Are you single at the present time? Do you have children at home? Are you married with children? Do you have paid employment of some kind involving, say, more than ten hours a week?

I hope that if you have the blessing of being a full-time homemaker, you know that it *is* a blessing to have circumstances that allow you to make that choice. Many women have made sacrifices to be full-time homemakers. You've heard many times from leaders of the Church how important and essential your work is, and I want to heartily second those statements.

But many women find themselves in different circumstances. I hope we can all accept each other's diverse circumstances and honor each other's decisions, even when they are different from the decisions we might have made, without judging or labeling. Many employed mothers are struggling with the problems of balancing children and careers, whether in two-parent or one-parent households. When we work and have children, we automatically have to juggle things. Both work and family seem to need to come first. They can take turns coming first if we're organized, and work very hard, and have good luck. At other times, we just have to muddle through.

But whether we're married or single, if we have children at home, there are a whole lot of other things that have to take second place. Let me use myself for an example. Ed and I both took our work very seriously, we took our parenting very seriously, and we took our Church callings very seriously. During the years when our boys were growing up, we made some decisions about what was nice and what was essential. Sunday meetings were essential. Firesides and study groups were nice. Hobbies that didn't include the children were nice, but not essential. Service projects our boys could do with us were essential. We put a high priority on school activities when the boys were home, but we didn't get to as many movies, plays, and concerts as some of our friends. We didn't feel bad about what we missed. Parenting is a very intensive obligation — and we gave it top priority — but it's a limited one. The children grow up. Then there's time to do something else.

One of our high priorities was finding the best care-givers, the best teachers, the best child-care situations we could; then we counted on these people to do their best with our boys. Of course we were always concerned. Doesn't part of your mind track each one of your children, whether it's the baby taking a nap or your third-grader's recess or your sixteen-year-old's play rehearsal? Still, knowing that they were being cared for by responsible, loving people freed us to take turns putting family and work first. We couldn't be with our boys and at work simultaneously. We couldn't do a good job at work if we were distracted and worried about what our sons were doing. Nor could we do a good job of parenting at home if we were distracted and worried about work. We set priorities. We organized together to find the best solution to our needs. And then we didn't worry.

Naturally, our priorities kept shifting. Ed and I both had many opportunities for community service in connection with our professional work. We had a policy between us. If one of us got an invitation to serve on a committee or attend a conference or join a task force—even if it was very important and something we knew we could make a contribution to—we always said, "I'll need to talk this over with my husband (or wife). Then I'll call you tomorrow." Then Ed and I would give this invitation some hard scrutiny. How much time would it really take? When and how often were the meetings? We turned down many things because we could see that we'd be spending too many evenings away from our boys or that one of us was already doing too much. It was easier to say no to such requests when we gave ourselves some time to think about them and talk together.

This advice applies even to callings in the Church. Church service brings its own blessings, but we will have many opportunities to serve throughout our lives, and a ward needs many different officers and teachers. I think it is very appropriate to share our life circumstances with someone who is issuing us a calling. Perhaps we have information that person needs about whether the calling will be good for us at that moment.

We all have received callings in the Church that we feel very comfortable with and others that really stretch our capacities. The person calling us should be able to tell us that he or she sought and received confirmation about our calling. We, in turn, have a right to have that inspiration confirmed to us. Sometimes it happens immediately, during the calling. Sometimes we need to ask for a little time to pray, think, and consult with our families about it.

Let me summarize what I'm saying about setting priorities and making choices. Only you know your circumstances, your energy level, the needs of your children, and the emotional demands of your other obligations. Be wise during intensive seasons of your life. Cherish your agency, and don't give it away casually. Don't compare yourself to others—nearly always this will make you despondent. Don't accept somebody else's interpretation of how you should be spending your time. Make the best decision you can and then evaluate it to see how it works. Practice saying, "I feel good about my decision to . . . " and then fill in the blank with whatever you've decided. If you find yourself saying, "I should feel good about this decision, but . . . " then perhaps you need to reevaluate that decision.

On one occasion I attended a meeting where someone was telling us about the importance of teaching women to strengthen the family. I had a little trouble with that presentation in three ways. First, that approach seems to assume that women are *weakening* the family. Of the hundreds of women I know, I don't know anybody who isn't doing the best she can to make her family strong. Second, I want to know if men are getting the same message. Men as a group certainly have far more control than women over many of the social and economic factors that make strong families possible. And third, I want a few reports from the real world about the specifics of family life. I don't think generalities are very helpful. Until those three conditions are met, the major product of sermons about strengthening the family is likely to be guilt, and I'm against guilt.

As I have stated earlier, I wonder if some wonderful Mormon mothers are missing out on much of the joy in motherhood because they have picked up unnecessary burdens. We need to make the best choices we can, with the guidance of the Spirit, and then lighten up!

One more thing about doing a good job with your family while you're working full-time: Respect the agency of your children. As a schoolteacher and a principal, I had a lot of contact with children of working parents. This can be a rough situation—or it can be one in which children can develop a lot of esteem, mature more rapidly, accept responsibilities, and feel like an important part of the family. Here's how the most successful parents made the experience work for them instead of against them:

First, they were very clear about their expectations. Second, they were consistent about following through. They said things such as, "Lonnie and Susan, this afternoon after school, I expect you to come straight home and make a sandwich for your snack. I'll call you about twenty minutes to four. Susan, you can play baseball with the neighborhood kids while Lonnie is watching 'Rescue Rangers,' but then both of you need to do your homework and practice the piano and flute. Lonnie, your chore is to take a package of hamburger out of the freezer and bring up a bottle of peaches from downstairs. Susan, your job is to put a load of light-colored clothes in the washing machine. Both of you put your cups in the dishwasher after your snack."

Then the phone call at 3:40 goes over these arrangements again, and when you get home at 5:30, you get another report, accompanied with lots of appreciation, hugs, and thanks all around.

Third, these parents made sharp distinctions between family time and work time. They didn't make many phone calls home on work time—and they didn't need to. They weren't worried about what their children were doing, because their children knew what they were supposed to do. If they had to take work home, they were clear with the children and renegotiated the schedule so that the children didn't feel dumped. These parents were also clear with their employers about their availability. They were available for real emergencies; but if an emergency developed simply because someone hadn't thought through what needed to happen, they were clear and firm, after it was over, about saying, "I can't effectively work like this, and I can't be on call every weekend. Since this report is due every quarter, then we need to set up earlier deadlines."

THE IMPORTANCE OF PRAYER

The way to literally open the door to the guest room and let Jesus come into other parts of your home—and your life—is through prayer. Paul told the Thessalonians to "pray without ceasing," and "in every thing give thanks." (1 Thessalonians 5:17–18.) Alma is even more specific: "Yea, and when you do not cry unto the Lord, let your hearts be full, drawn out in prayer unto him continually for your welfare, and also for the welfare of those who are around you." (Alma 34:27.)

To me, this means one thing. Our Heavenly Father wants us to live a Savior-centered life. He wants our sense of the Savior as a real person to fill our consciousness. He wants us to take seriously that promise about the constant companionship of the Holy Ghost. And this, in turn, means that Heavenly

182

Father doesn't want to hear only "nice" prayers. He wants to hear real prayers, honest prayers. How many times are our evening prayers just one more chore? Scoop up the evening paper and put it away, jot "celery salt" on the shopping list, collect that dirty sock for the hamper, brush your teeth, and drop to your knees. We all know how to say prayers. We know the polite formula of "we thank thee for the gospel, we ask thee to bless the missionaries . . . "

But who are we trying to kid? Jesus has just seen the stove where the spaghetti boiled over, and it was pretty obvious that wasn't the only thing that had ever boiled over on that stove. He heard what you muttered when you picked up that one sock, just as you've been doing for the past eight years. He caught that worry about the dentist bill that flashed across your mind when you were putting toothpaste on your brush. He doesn't want polite platitudes. He wants you! All of you! He wants to be the center of your total life—the worried you, the mad you, and the sad you as well as the inspired, happy, obedient, loving you.

Christie Ann Giles, a sister missionary, wrote a wonderful essay about how she discovered this principle. It was her second night at the Missionary Training Center, and she was miserable:

> I didn't like my companion, I didn't like Spanish, and I didn't like myself much for being such a baby.
>
> I started my prayer, but then realized that I didn't have anything to say. Although I desperately needed someone to talk to, it just didn't seem right to express my empty, lonely, and bitter feelings to Heavenly Father. I finally said a standard, "thank you for my health and the chance to be here," sort of prayer and crawled into bed.

Why doesn't Heavenly Father help me? If he really knows how I feel before I ask, what is he waiting for? I thought angrily.

Then I remembered the book of Enos, which I had read that afternoon. . . . His words echoed in my mind: "I did pour out my whole soul unto God." (Enos 1:9.) Had I done the same? . . . I knew I hadn't.

I knelt again. This time I had plenty to say. I told my Father how frustrated I felt, how I couldn't learn the language, how I needed to love my companion, and how I wanted to do a good job. I cried as I explained that I felt abandoned, and I needed his help. . . .

This time, I didn't say a prayer—I prayed. ("A Change of Heart," *New Era*, November 1991, p. 11.)

When it comes to prayer, let's have no more empty statements and insincere but polite phrases. Be honest. If you're mad, say so. If you're confused, say so. And don't think anything is too small for the Savior's loving attention. Catherine Marshall, who has written many profound and thoughtful reflections on the dailiness of living, tells a story I love about this very principle:

In a woman's magazine I had seen a picture of an hourglass-shaped curtain, so attractive that I decided to copy it. It looked easy, but I soon discovered that when I pulled the curtain together in the middle, the rods bowed at top and bottom.

I worked and struggled without any success to figure it out. Some sort of mathematical problem seemed to be involved, and I am not good at mathematics! I grew more and more exasperated at my own stupidity. How silly to be nonplussed by such a small problem!

Then I called a friend in, but she could not solve it either.

Finally, in great disgust, I gave up, went upstairs, and flopped down on a bed. After I had been lying there a few minutes, the inner Voice said very quietly, "You do it this way." There followed a set of simple directions involving graduated tucks. The directions worked easily, perfectly.

Does this seem trivial? Of course it is. . . . [But] most of our days are full of ordinary events and common experiences. Are we to believe that God has no interest in these? (*Beyond Our Selves* [New York: McGraw-Hill, 1961], pp. 135–36.)

The Savior calls us to do two things — to come to him, and to open the door to our hearts and let him come to us. The Apostle Paul, struggling for words to express how complete our access is, says: "For I am persuaded, that neither death, nor life, nor angels, nor principalities, nor powers, nor things present, nor things to come, nor height, nor depth, nor any other creature, shall be able to separate us from the love of God, which is in Christ Jesus our Lord." (Romans 8:38–39.)

Think of the power and joy that come into our lives when we face our days and our nights with Jesus beside us. We can deal with adversity because Christ has been there before us, experiencing all that we experience, and being with us in our trials. We can make wise choices and set good priorities, knowing that our "no" is as important as our "yes" when he is with us. If we will let him, he will accompany us daily and hourly instead of being stuck in the back room, waiting patiently until we can snatch a few minutes to dash back and be with him. We can be free of guilt because he does not condemn us. On the contrary, he is our advocate. He stands ready, knocking and calling, ready to respond to the three-second prayer of our heart as well as to the longer pleadings on our knees. He is ready to heal us and make us whole. He desires our happiness and promises us his joy.

May we be Savior-centered, knowing that we are beloved of him. May we be true transmitters of that love to others, and truly his sisters and brothers in service. What openness of heart and fullness of joy await us!

CHAPTER FIFTEEN

# Spiritual Preparation

ONE OF THE MOST BEAUTIFUL VERSES in all scripture having to do with preparation is the Lord's loving promise to his apostles on the eve of his crucifixion: "Let not your heart be troubled: ye believe in God, believe also in me. In my Father's house are many mansions: if it were not so, I would have told you. I go to prepare a place for you. And if I go and prepare a place for you, I will come again, and receive you unto myself; that where I am, there ye may be also. And whither I go ye know, and the way ye know." (John 14:1–4.)

Isn't that a beautiful promise? When it comes to spiritual preparation, the Lord has been before us, preparing the way. Even now, he has a place prepared for us in the mansions of his Father. Sometimes we may feel terribly unprepared spiritually. Remember that he says, "and the way ye know." Even before we entered this sphere of mortality, he had prepared mansions for us. If he has so much confidence in our spiritual strength, surely we can lean on his faith in us if our faith in him seems lacking for a moment.

TODAY PREPARES FOR TOMORROW

Today prepares for tomorrow. Think about that for a minute. Preparation is a *present* activity.

We often visualize preparation only in terms of some dramatic future test. We prepare food storage because there might be a calamity—a flood, a fire, a nuclear war, or unemployment that tests our financial capability. We prepare through our education for the test of finding and keeping employment. We take childbirth preparation classes to get ready for delivery. We fast, pray, read the scriptures, serve, and build our faith in the Savior in preparation for some future trial—perhaps when a husband dies or a child goes astray and our faith will be needed to withstand the test or reclaim the child.

You can probably see where this is headed. No, that's not really *why* we do any of these things. These spectacular crises may or may not come. We all hope they won't; and even with our best preparation, we're not sure how we will act when they do. But a life centered in the future is not really the kind of life that makes living today worthwhile. It ignores and invalidates the claims of the present.

I believe Heavenly Father arranged mortality for us so that we could experience being in only one place at a time and thinking only one thought at a time. This way, we would have to really, seriously choose. On a given day you could have dozens of perfectly worthy options from which to choose. You could be reshingling the house, or taking the LSAT test to enter law school. You could be planting the garden or having lunch with a friend. All of these things are good things. But you must choose. We can only live in the present, not the past or the future.

So what are our *present* reasons for doing these worthy things I've just mentioned? I think a better reason for storing food is that it gives us flexibility and increased options in our individual homes—in terms of both unexpected company on Tuesday night and unexpected crises. We seek education, not primarily for future employment—although that is certainly one valid reason—but because of the very real daily joy of stretching our minds and learning. And we study the scriptures for the spiritual strength that comes from them, pray daily for the joy of ongoing communication with our Heavenly Father, serve those around us for the delight and happiness it brings to be part of a community that loves each other, and renew our covenants at sacrament meeting and in the temple for the increased clarity and steadying that they give us.

I love Ephesians 6:15: "[Have] your feet shod with the *preparation* of the gospel of peace." For me, the gospel brings peace. Even when it stretches us and makes us work hard, it brings peace. With peace in our hearts, we're prepared for anything.

Let me relate a story that illustrates the attitude I think we should have toward this kind of preparation. You know the toy that is a wooden paddle with a ball attached to it by an elastic band? There was a time when I struggled to be able to even once hit that ball with that paddle. My grip was feeble. I had undergone a mastectomy for cancer, followed by several weeks of radiation therapy. During my recuperation, for about six weeks part of my physical therapy was to hit this ball with the paddle to build up the muscles under my arm. I also practiced squeezing a ball in my hands. Another exercise was spider-walking my fingers up the wall three times a day, with the goal of getting my hand above my head.

I didn't know if I would ever be able to lift my arm above my head. I remember trying to spider-walk on the wall and marking how high I got. At first, I felt that my arm wouldn't move at all and I would stretch and stretch to make my middle fingernail slide as high as I could make it go — just like a first-grader standing as tall as he can when he's being measured — so that I could be just a hair's breadth ahead of my last score. Sometimes I marked progress by one-eighth of an inch. Then I cheered for myself, saying, "Wow! I made progress!" Sometimes there wasn't any progress at all and I'd say to myself, "That's okay. Just wait until I try it again at noon." What a celebration when I made a whole inch! And at the end of six weeks, I could get my arm up above my head. Now I can lift anything, turn it in any direction, move without thinking about it.

I wasn't "preparing" to lift my arm above my head when I came home from the hospital. That was a goal that was simply beyond me. I was preparing at noon to do better than I had that morning. I was preparing at night to do better than I had at noon. And bit by bit, the goal came, too.

Preparation occurs daily and fits us to live in the present, as well as in the future.

SPIRITUALITY—NOT A PROGRAM

The second point I'd like to make is that spiritual strength is personal. It's individual. It's part of our lives that doesn't belong to a Church program. The Church can put us in good places where we have increased opportunities to build our spirituality, but the Church can't make it happen for us if we don't take advantage of those opportunities.

Soon after our youngest son, Robert, entered the mission field, he wrote home, "I've been asking myself why I'm here in the mission field, and I think I know why. Before I came, I think I was physically, mentally, and emotionally well prepared—not only for my mission but for life in general. I had things in pretty good balance. But now I realize that I was not spiritually prepared as well as I should be. My mission is teaching me things about spirituality that I would not have known otherwise."

Ed and I were thrilled to get that letter. Robert was always a son we were proud of. We didn't worry about him or see deficiencies in him. But we saw in his experience a wonderful dimension of self-awareness and a hunger for growth that assured us he was on the right track.

Since his return, we've seen that the spiritual progress he made on his mission has been permanent. He was always kind, thoughtful, and willing to serve others. He has had many leadership and teaching opportunities, but we're much prouder of the fact that he actively and quietly seeks out opportunities for service. He doesn't care too much about positions, and he gets pretty impatient sometimes with those gigantic checklists of 212 things every Mormon is supposed to do every month. But if someone needs him, he's there.

For example, once Ed and I were visiting him and our daughter-in-law in Milwaukee, and he excused himself for a couple of hours. "Somebody's moving out of the ward and I need to go help," he explained. After he left, Chris, our daughter-in-law, commented, "Sometimes he's the only one there, but he always helps. He's very sensitive to the needs of others."

That's spiritual strength, service that doesn't come by assignment or in relation to a position, but that springs from the kind of character Robert has. I know that he remembers an experience we had in one ward because we've laughed about it as a family many times. The bishop announced that we needed to have a ward work party to clean up the grounds around the chapel. When the time came, only seven people were there: The bishop, Ed and I, our two sons, a fairly elderly gentleman, and a teenage boy.

The bishop asked, "Why aren't more people here?"

The teenager said, "Would you be here, if you weren't the bishop?"

The bishop laughed and laughed—and just shook his head. "You may have a point there, son," he said.

For me the point is that being a good Christian is a Church job all by itself. We don't have to be perfect. In fact, I think I can assure you that we won't be perfect. But we can try for progress. We can respond to needs kindly, responsibly, sensitively. We don't need to berate ourselves for failing to see a need or for failing to respond to it perfectly or for failing to respond to all the needs we see. It's okay to measure our progress by an eighth of an inch.

Janet Griffin Lee, speaking at the 1990 BYU Women's Conference, talked about this very point:

"Perhaps we misunderstand the scriptures that admonish us to 'Be ye therefore perfect.' Do we think that perfection needs to be attained immediately — in fact, right now? We set off at a relentless, impossible pace. Do we expect to arrive at perfection in this life? Maybe tomorrow, if we hurry? . . .

"I evaluate myself on a continuum rather than in absolutes. . . . I concentrate on what I accomplished, focusing on one single aspect in my life where I am making progress. . . . Once I have done that, I then ignore the fact that the wonderful meal I was going to prepare was replaced by Campbell's soup and toast. I stop thinking about how I missed my five-mile run in the morning and concentrate on the time I spent with a dear friend." (*Women and the Power Within*, p. 139.)

Isn't that wise? Isn't that wonderful? Sister Ardeth Kapp expressed a similar sentiment: "Sometimes we feel that we need to do it all — and all at once. But that is not the case. When we give what we have according to our time, according to our energy, according to where we are at this moment in our development, then the Lord will take what we have to offer and he will make up the difference. That is the grace of God." (*Women and the Power Within*, p. 46.)

SPIRITUALITY IS INDIVIDUAL

My third point is closely related to the second: In addition to being incremental — one bit at a time — and progressive, spirituality is also individual. Yes, there are ways in which it's collective, too. I think we've all felt the strength of fasting and praying as a ward — perhaps for someone who is ill, perhaps to end a drought, perhaps to contribute to the Ethiopian Relief Fund. But the point that I want to make here is that what builds your spirituality may be different from what builds someone else's.

At the same BYU Women's Conference mentioned earlier, Marybeth Raynes, a marriage and family therapist with a terrific sense of humor, said, "One difference between rats and humans is that in a maze, once the rat discovers a blind alley, it does not go down that blind alley a second time. Humans, however, will continue indefinitely going down the same blind alley, especially if the entry to that alley is labeled, 'This is the way it should be.' " (*Women and the Power Within*, p. 184.)

Maybe you've received a lot of "shoulds" and "oughts" about your spiritual life. Do any of these sound familiar?

You should read the scriptures at the same time every day.

You should go to the temple once a month.

You should always wait quietly for an answer after you've prayed.

You should always accept every calling in the Church.

Well, I have another "should" for you. Here it is. Are you ready?

You should do what works for *you*.

It's okay to consult your own needs and wants. Growth comes when we feel ourselves drawn in certain directions, when we feel unsatisfied needs in ourselves and reach out to meet those needs in righteous ways. Maybe what we need is the discipline of spending a whole uninterrupted half-hour every day reading the scriptures. Or maybe it's our season of life where we really need to interact with little children so intensively that scripture study means reading one scripture card stuck on the mirror while we're brushing our teeth.

It's okay to ask yourself what you need and what you want. Here are some questions to replace those "shoulds" and "oughts."

"What do I want out of my attendance at church? Am I getting it?"

"If I could have any calling in the ward, what would it be?" or "If I didn't have any Church callings right now, what kind of service would I rather be doing?"

"What kinds of experiences with the scriptures have brought me the most joy in the past, or been most satisfying to me? Is there a way to have those experiences more regularly?"

"What kind of a prayer life do I have? Are there moments or levels of quietness where I can hear the still small voice of the Holy Ghost? Do I consciously invite the Holy Ghost to 'come along' in my daily activities?"

This last question is an interesting one. Do you feel that the Holy Ghost is interested in what you're doing, whether you're walking to class, tending your baby, talking to another employee at work, or really digging into that closet that's needed cleaning for ten years? Obviously, the Holy Ghost will depart from the presence of sin, but all too often we feel that the Holy Ghost only shows up for church and disappears Monday through Saturday. That's not true. Monday through Saturday is where we live our lives, and our confirmation promise was for the constant companionship of the Holy Ghost. Maybe if we're not feeling the Holy Ghost more often, it's because we're the ones who walk out of sacrament meeting to the parking lot and say, "Well, see you next week."

Spirituality is individual. Find things that work for you as you develop spiritual strength. Our Heavenly Father has not just one mansion but "many mansions." I don't think he expects us all to find spiritual strength in exactly the same ways. Find out what works for you and then follow it.

## ACCEPTING OUR SEASONS

The fourth point I'd like to make is that we need to accept our seasons gracefully. Different seasons make different demands and teach different lessons. I turned sixty-six the year Relief Society turned 150, so I'm very aware of the lessons that this stage of my life has to teach me. Ed and I thought we would enjoy a leisurely retirement—do a lot of temple work, perhaps serve another mission as long as it wasn't too strenuous, travel, visit our children, maybe take up a new hobby or two. If nothing else, I've learned flexibility and adaptability. There's always a surprise around the corner. And sometimes many surprises.

Perhaps this is your season for community involvement. I am thrilled by the ways our sisters reach out to their towns, their school boards, their professional associations, and their community organizations. Do you know that you are moving forward in response to prophecy? The Relief Society and the Young Women's Mutual Improvement Association were both charter members of the National Council of Women when it was organized in the 1880s. Belle S. Spafford, when she was general president of the Relief Society, was elected president of the National Council of Women. She wrote:

"As I looked out at the glittering audience made up of people of many nations . . . my mind suddenly flashed back to the words of our pioneer leaders at which Sister Sharp [my counselor] and I had smiled—' . . . standing as we do at the head of the women of the world . . . for the rights of the women of Zion and the rights of the women of all nations.'

"This night in that far-away northern country [of Finland], I did not smile. I knew that our pioneer women leaders had been given by divine insight a knowledge of the destiny of Relief Society. . . . It is my conviction that the time had come for Relief Society's influence to be felt worldwide among womankind." (*A Woman's Reach* [Salt Lake City: Deseret Book, 1974], p. 98.)

As Sister Spafford predicted, women of the Church have steadily and steadfastly worked for peace, against poverty, for justice, and against ignorance all over the world. In 1979, President Spencer W. Kimball prophesied: "Much of the major growth that is coming to the Church in the last days will come because many of the good women of the world (in whom there is often such an inner sense of spirituality) will be drawn to the Church in large numbers. This will happen to the degree that the women of the Church reflect righteousness and artic- ulateness in their lives and to the degree that the women of the Church are seen as distinct and different—in happy ways." ("The Role of Righteous Women," *Ensign*, November 1979, pp. 103–4.)

Those pioneer women, who envisioned their female leaders standing at the head of all womankind, had a glorious vision of what their united spiritual strength could do. Sister Spafford articulated that same vision, and President Kimball prophesied the hunger of the world for that vision.

We are building our spiritual strength every day in little ways, ways as little as trying to reach an eighth of an inch higher at noon than we did in the morning. We need to listen to our own hearts and spirits and feed them what they need most to grow on. We need to accept the tasks and opportunities ex- tended to us by each season of our lives.

But most of all, we need to remember that we need not be troubled in our hearts, for Jesus has prepared the way. He has promised us that we will know the way as we walk in it. And he is waiting for us to come to the mansion that he has prepared for us. He is the great measure of reality, against which other measures crumble. When his light burns in our hearts, no darkness can smother it. When he is beside us, no enemy can threaten us.

Corrie Ten Boom, a wonderful Dutch woman, was imprisoned in Ravensbruck during World War II with her sister, Betsie, for sheltering Jews in their home. She writes this touching vignette:

> Whenever large numbers of our Dutch women were sent away on transports, they were replaced by Polish women. These women had suffered a great deal and looked worn and anxious. We could not understand each other's language. Yet we suffered the same affliction side by side. The same Saviour had borne their griefs also.
>
> It was evening. A little woman was leaning wearily against the edge of her bed. She looked deeply unhappy. Betsie went to her, took her hand in her own, and said questioningly, "Jesocs Christoes?"
>
> A glow of happiness came over the face of the little woman. She drew Betsie to her and kissed her. The Name that is above every name united not only heaven and earth, but also the hearts of people of different tongues. These Polish Catholic women had such great love for their Saviour that the sound of His spoken name made their faces shine.
>
> We sometimes sang, "Come to the Saviour, make no delay," and they would sing it with us. The melody of that song had been imported from Poland by the Salvation Army [to Holland]. What the words were in Polish, I did not know. Someday we shall sing that song before the throne of God, and there will be no difference of language to separate us. (A Prisoner and Yet . . . [New York: Jove Publications, 1977], pp. 131–32.)

Our strength is in the Lord. There may be no enormous tests in our lives, against which we will match our preparation in a David-and-Goliath contest. But each day, we are preparing for tomorrow. Let us rejoice in our blessings of today, and find our spiritual strength in the Lord and Savior who died for us, who lives in us, and who also lives in anticipation of that meeting before his Father's throne.

# CHAPTER SIXTEEN

# "Learn of Me"

THE THEME FOR ONE OF THE Relief Society Study Guides is "Learn of Me," taken from a beautiful promise in the Doctrine and Covenants: "Learn of me, and listen to my words, walk in the meekness of my Spirit, and you shall have peace in me." (D&C 19:23.) These words give me the feeling of such closeness to, such intimacy with the Savior, looking at him, listening to him, learning from him, walking with him, and feeling his peace like his very arms around me. Within each of us is an intense hunger for this intimacy with and closeness to him. I think we all want to feel his spirit around us.

I've thought for a long time about what we are supposed to learn of him. I've asked myself, "Chieko, what is it that *you* have learned of him? And how have you learned it?"

I find myself coming back to the same answer. It's more of an image than a concept. The image that comes to mind is one of light. Jesus calls himself the "light of the world" and promises, "he that followeth me shall not walk in darkness, but shall have the light of life." (John 8:12.) The scriptures are inundated with this light. The following are just a few of my favorites:

Paul, in writing to the Romans, said, "The night is far spent, the day is at hand: let us therefore cast off the works of darkness, and let us put on the armour of light." (Romans 13:12.)

Paul told the Thessalonians: "Ye are all the children of light, and the children of the day: we are not of the night, nor of darkness." (1 Thessalonians 5:5.)

Speaking to the modern Saints, the Lord said: "That which is of God is light; and he that receiveth light, and continueth in God, receiveth more light; and that light groweth brighter and brighter until the perfect day." (D&C 50:24.)

Isaiah, describing the millennial day we all long for, said, "The sun shall be no more thy light by day; neither for brightness shall the moon give light unto thee: but the Lord shall be unto thee an everlasting light, and thy God thy glory." (Isaiah 60:19.)

The Psalmist rejoices, "The Lord is my light and my salvation." (Psalm 27:1.)

And then there is the marvelous section in the Doctrine and Covenants that knits together the physical light of the sun and moon with the spiritual light of Christ. It describes "the light of truth" and reminds us, "This is the light of Christ. As also he is in the sun, and the light of the sun, and the power thereof by which it was made. . . . And the light which shineth, which giveth you light, is through him who enlighteneth your eyes, which is the same light that quickeneth your understandings; which light proceedeth forth from the presence of God to fill the immensity of space—the light which is in all things, which giveth life to all things, which is the law by which all things are governed." (D&C 88:6–7, 11–13.)

There are two things I want us to remember about light: First, light doesn't compete with darkness. It dispels darkness. And second, Christ's burden is light.

First, think about the contrast between light and darkness. Light doesn't compete with darkness. Suppose you're in a dark room and you want to get rid of the darkness. You can't catch the darkness and put it in a box. You can't sweep it out the

200

door. You can't find a hole that the darkness is coming in through and nail a board over it. It really doesn't work to decide, "I can live with this darkness. It's my darkness, after all. In fact, dark is beautiful." And we reach the point of the ridiculous if we get more people involved – organize a committee to study the darkness, as it were. The more you grapple with the dark, the further away you are from getting rid of it. Only light dispels darkness. Darkness and light can't occupy the same space. And don't forget Okazaki chapter one, verse one, "Lighten up!"

As Alma the Younger lay unconscious for three days and nights following the angel's visit to him, he came to understand the spiritual consequences of his particular kind of darkness. This experience filled him with such "inexpressible horror" that his one desire was to "be banished and become extinct both soul and body, that I might not be brought to stand in the presence of my God, to be judged of my deeds."

In this tormenting experience, he remembered his father's testimony of Jesus Christ, who would "atone for the sins of the world." His "mind caught hold upon this thought" – perhaps something like a drowning person seizing a log that floats by. He cried out to Jesus to have mercy on him in his great darkness, and the darkness vanished. Alma says: "I could remember my pains no more; yea, I was harrowed up by the memory of my sins no more. And oh, what joy, and what marvelous light [there's that word again] I did behold; yea, my soul was filled with joy as exceeding as was my pain!" (Alma 36:14–20.)

Alma discovered how to bring light into his life! He learned that alone he was powerless to dispel his own darkness, but that the simple act of calling on Jesus made it vanish. If there's darkness in your life, don't grapple with it, don't dwell on it, don't stay involved in it. Get to the light switch! The Lord tells us, "Know the truth, that you may chase darkness from among you." (D&C 50:25.)

When I was about seven years old, electricity came to our village. We had a refrigerator—an icebox with a square hole in which to put the big chunks of ice that were delivered every week by a truck that bounced and maneuvered over rutted dirt roads from the nearest town, seven or eight miles away. My father was a progressive man, a man of great faith. When he heard that electricity was coming, he took some of the money he and Mother had saved from working on the plantation and bought a little refrigerator. Men came, strung wires from the poles to our house, installed wall sockets, and hung from the ceilings lengths of flex wiring that dangled down with sockets at the ends. They screwed a light bulb into one of the sockets, pulled on the string, and said, "Now it's ready for the electricity and it's on. When the current is connected, you'll see the light come on." They showed us how to plug in the refrigerator and said, "On Tuesday night at eight o'clock, the current will be connected and you'll have electricity in your house."

When Tuesday night came, none of us children went out to play, and my father didn't go fishing, either. We all sat around in a circle in the light of the kerosene lantern on the table. I had polished the glass chimney of that lamp that morning and trimmed the wick, just as I did every day; but there were already little black specks settling on the chimney and I knew I was going to have to clean it again the next day. I could hardly understand what the men meant by electricity coming to our house. But we sat there and waited.

As our wind-up alarm clock ticked closer to eight o'clock, we stopped fidgeting and stared at the light bulb. It seemed a long way up there, in the dim light from our kerosene lamp. And the refrigerator stood quietly next to the icebox. We could hear the drops of water from the melting ice quietly splat into the drip tray.

And then it was eight o'clock, and the light came on! I stared at it with my mouth open, this light that sprang from nowhere and made the room so much brighter than the lamp had. In the silence, I heard the refrigerator motor turn over and then begin to purr quietly to itself. I still remember that marvelous, dazzling moment. Electricity had come to our house and it had changed everything.

For all of us — whether we are converts or were born in the Church — there comes a moment when the gospel becomes real to us in a way that it hasn't been before. These are moments of a reality beyond realness. They make a light go on permanently, a light that never goes off unless a line goes down or a switch gets turned off somewhere. If that's the light that we share together when we feast on the scriptures and learn of Christ, then it is a light that dispels the darkness in our lives.

The second idea follows the first naturally: Christ's burden is light. When he says, "Learn of me," he wants us to do something that will be light and joyful to us, not heavy and discouraging.

We are all hungry to learn of Jesus. We want the spiritual food that the gospel offers us. When the scriptures tell us to "press forward, feasting upon the word of Christ" (2 Nephi 31:20), that's the kind of spiritual food we need to sustain us. We can meet an important part of those needs with our own study of the scriptures. But there are times when we want to feast together — not a solitary sandwich, even if it's a delicious one, but a banquet in which we all share. I'd like to think of such meetings as Relief Society and Sunday School as providing these banquets.

We can come to church hungry to learn about Jesus, hungry for spiritual nourishment; and leaders can see that there is spiritual food by calling teachers who know and love Jesus. I love this scripture from John 5:35 in which Jesus describes John the Baptist: "[John] was a burning and a shining light: and ye were willing for a season to rejoice in his light." We need teachers who are burning and shining lights.

Sometimes people confuse spirituality with solemnity. It's been my experience that one of the inevitable effects of true spirituality is light-heartedness, a generosity in happiness. Joy is even more contagious than chicken pox! If you knew that every Sunday you were going to be bathed in the radiance of testimonies of the Savior, could wild horses keep you away from church? Hardly!

Jesus issued a stirring invitation to each of us: "Come unto me, all ye that labour and are heavy laden, and I will give you rest. Take my yoke upon you, and learn of me; for I am meek and lowly in heart: and ye shall find rest unto your souls. For my yoke is easy, and my burden is light." (Matthew 11:28–30.)

But how can this be? If we are already burdened, how will taking yet another burden—a heavy yoke—upon us give us rest? And how can his burden be "light"?

Jesus is our yokemate. When we take *his* yoke upon us, he's pulling in the other half of the yoke. There aren't many loads that are too heavy to pull if Jesus is pulling beside us.

If we're really feeling burdened, then maybe we're not carrying Jesus' yoke. Maybe we're carrying somebody else's. Maybe it's time to say to ourselves, "I really feel dragged down when I hear _____" (you can fill in the blank with whatever happens to fit: "that I should be doing genealogy," "that I should be reading the scriptures for half an hour every day," "that I should be doing more visiting teaching," and so forth).

Instead, try this. Say to yourself, "This is how I really, truly, honestly feel. It's a burden, and I'm not going to carry it any longer." And then dump it! Just twitch your shoulders and let it slide to the ground. Why don't you practice this shoulder twitch I'm talking about; can you feel the burdens sliding off right now? Think of this as an exercise in lightening up!

Can you feel how differently your heart feels when you let go of unnecessary burdens? Isn't there a lightness and a brightness that wasn't there before? When you do this shoulder twitch, give yourself a few days to get used to the feeling. And then think if there's maybe somebody else you should tell about it.

Maybe you should talk to the Relief Society president if you find yourself coming to Relief Society week after week and feeling no relief—instead, just more burdens. Jesus had situations like this in mind, I think, when he said, "What man is there of you, whom if his son ask bread, will he give him a stone? Or if he ask a fish, will he give him a serpent?" (Matthew 7:9–10.) Let me phrase it like this: "What Relief Society president is there among you, who, if a sister ask for comfort, will give her a lecture? Or, if she ask for more spiritually nourishing lessons, will give her guilt instead?"

Or maybe there's someone else you should talk to. The next time the teacher has this big package of "shoulds" that she wants to hand you, might you raise your hand in class and politely decline to take it from her? Typically we just sit there and let her put it in our laps, because we don't want to hurt her feelings or give other people the idea that we aren't as spiritual or capable as they are. And we usually think we're the only person in that room having trouble carrying the ton plus ten pounds that we're already sinking under.

But maybe there's another sister in the room who needs to hear you say you're not going to pick up that burden. Maybe that would give her the courage to say, "My goodness, I feel the same way! Hearing this really made me feel unhappy and heavy. But maybe I don't have to carry this burden either."

We still want to enjoy a unified sisterhood, though, so we need to find a way to talk like sisters when we raise our hands in class. I'd suggest two different ways. One is to phrase your point like a question, for instance, "Do you mean that each of us, no matter our circumstances, should be doing genealogy every week?" Sometimes that helps the teacher think about how what she has said could be interpreted. The second way is to talk to the teacher the same way you talk to yourself when you're figuring out how you feel. For example: "When I hear you say that we should all be doing genealogy every week, it makes me feel terribly burdened and oppressed. I'm glad your circumstances allow you to spend an afternoon a week doing research at the branch family history library, but mine don't. I'd like to hear some suggestions about how people in my circumstances can do genealogy."

If Jesus wants us to carry a particular yoke, he will find a way to make it light for us. Do we believe him? Do we believe what he tells us?

When we encounter burdens too heavy to carry alone, our only source of permanent strength is to yoke ourselves to Christ. But do we believe him? Do we believe what he tells us? Stephen E. Robinson, a professor of ancient scripture at BYU, explained the power of the Atonement in the following way:

> Now, to have faith in Jesus Christ is not merely to believe that he is who he says he is, or to believe *in* Christ. Sometimes, to have faith in Christ is also to *believe* Christ. Both as a bishop and as a teacher in the Church, I have learned there are many who believe Jesus is the Son of God and that he is the Savior of the World, but they do not believe that he can save them. They believe in his identity, but not in

his power to cleanse and to purify and to save. To have faith in his identity is only half the principle. To have faith in his ability and in his power to cleanse and to save, that is the other half. We must not only believe in Christ, we must *believe* Christ when he says, "I can cleanse you and make you celestial." ("Believing Christ: A Practical Approach to the Atonement," *BYU Today*, November 1990, p. 26.)

He tells about an experience his wife, Janet, had when they were living in Pennsylvania:

> Things were going pretty well; I'd been promoted. It was a good year for us as a family, though a trying year for Janet personally. That year she had our fourth child, graduated from college, passed the CPA exam, and was made Relief Society president. [Are you saying, "Good grief," just like I am right now?] We had temple recommends, and we held family home evening. I was serving in the bishopric. . . . Then one night the lights went out. Something happened in my wife that I can only describe as "dying spiritually." She wouldn't talk about it or tell me what was wrong. That was the worst part. For a couple of weeks she did not wish to participate in spiritual things, and she asked to be released from her callings.
>
> Finally, after about two weeks, one night I made her mad, and it came out. She said, "All right. You want to know what's wrong? I'll tell you what's wrong. I can't do it anymore. I can't lift it. I can't get up at 5:30 in the morning and bake bread and sew clothes and help my kids with their homework and do my own homework and do my Relief Society stuff and get my genealogy done and write the congressman and go to the PTA meetings and write the missionaries . . . " And she just started naming off one brick after another that had been laid on her, explaining all the things she could not do—a catalog of her flaws and imperfections. . . . "I've tried and I've tried, but I cannot keep all

of the commandments all the time." ("Believing Christ," p. 27.)

Have you ever had these feelings? You can imagine how relieved Brother Robinson felt, considering all the things he had imagined might have been the problem during those two terrible weeks. He explained to his wife that she "was trying to save herself with Jesus as an advisor. But we can't do that. . . . Of course we fail at the celestial level. That's why we need a savior, and why we are commanded to approach God and to call upon him so we may receive *according to our desires.*" ("Believing Christ," p. 29.) We don't have to be perfect. We just have to hunger and thirst for righteousness. The Atonement makes up that gap between what we are and what we need to be.

Kira Pratt Davis, who served a mission in Holland, wrote about meeting a man while she was tracting who obviously hated Mormons, hated Americans, and hated religion in general. He accused the missionaries of trying to sell God the way McDonald's sold hamburgers. He did not get angry at them, but there was something in the way he talked to them that was worse than anger. "It was cold-blooded," she says. "It was pure hate; it was evil." When they left, she says, "I felt as if I had struggled with someone trying to drown me. He had held my head under water in spite of my hitting and kicking and all that I could do, and I had begun to drown." They climbed on their bicycles and went home crying. After she and her companion prayed together, she went into the bedroom and said her own prayer:

> I wanted to know if I were the only crazy person in the world; I wanted to know if it was worth it to be out here, spilling my guts out; I wanted to know what God thought of me—if I was really as worthless a piece of trash as this man had made me feel. And as I prayed, I did see myself; I

saw a silly, vain, and intense person who had gone on a mission largely to prove that she wasn't just anybody. I saw how smart I thought I was. I saw myself posing and struggling, in my own way, for everyone, all the time. I cried, but at the same time, I felt a kind of solid earth beneath my soul, a bedrock reassurance that He regarded me kindly and saw all of what I was, but that it did not matter, as if his love were some low, constant, . . . pervasive humming, undisturbed by my falseness in the treble. It was a surprising answer. I had expected to be reassured that I was not all *that* bad. Instead, I realized that I *was* all that bad—but that God's feeling for me was not because *I* was good, but because *he* was good. ("God for $ale," *Exponent II*, April 1991, p. 8.)

I can't read that experience without seeing God with a twinkle in his eye, saying, "Lighten up, Kira! Why do you think I love you?" It is in the goodness of God, not in the goodness of ourselves, that our hope of the Atonement lies. We must have faith in Christ—not only that he is *the* Savior, but that he is *our* Savior.

Stephen Robinson told another story that impressed me. His seven-year-old daughter Sarah asked for a bicycle. She was the only child on the block without one. Brother Robinson didn't have enough money to buy her a bicycle at the time, so he sidestepped the issue by telling her, "You save all your pennies, and pretty soon you'll have enough for a bike." A couple of weeks later, he saw her do a job for Janet, then add the two pennies she earned to some others in a little jar with a slit in the lid. She showed him the pennies in the bottom and said, "You promised me that if I saved all my pennies, pretty soon I'd have enough for a bike. And, Daddy, I've saved every single one of them."

"My heart melted," he says. "She was doing everything in her power to follow my instructions." She didn't know—though he did—that she *would* eventually have enough pennies for a bicycle, but by then she would be in high school. So he took her shopping and they spent all afternoon looking at bicycles:

> Finally we found it—the *perfect* bicycle, the one she knew in the premortal existence. She got up on that bike, and she was thrilled. She then saw the price tag, reached down, and turned it over. When she saw how much it cost, her face fell and she started to cry. She said, "Oh, Dad, I'll never have enough for a bicycle."
>
> So I said, "Sarah, how much do you have?"
>
> She answered, "Sixty-one cents."
>
> "I'll tell you what," I said. "You give me everything you've got and a hug and a kiss, and the bike is yours." Well, she's never been stupid. She gave me a hug and a kiss. She gave me the sixty-one cents. Then I had to drive home very slowly because she wouldn't get off the bike. She rode home on the sidewalk, and . . . I drove along slowly beside her.

Brother Robinson tells what he learned from this experience:

> We all want something desperately—but it isn't a bicycle. We want the celestial kingdom. We want to be with our Father in Heaven. And no matter how hard we try, we come up short. At some point we realize, "I can't do this!"
>
> That was the point my wife, Janet, had reached. It is at that point that the sweetness of the gospel covenant comes to our taste as the Savior proposes, "I'll tell you what. All right, you're not perfect. How much do you have? What can you do? Where are you now? Give me all you've got, and I'll pay the rest. Give me a hug and a kiss; that is, enter into a personal relationship with me, and I will do what remains undone."

There is good news and bad news here. The bad news is that he still requires our best effort. We must try, we must work—we must do all that we can. But the good news is that having done all we can, it is enough. ("Believing Christ," pp. 51–52.)

Jesus bore the heaviest burden of all—the sins of all of us. He still bears that burden, and he is still the light of the world. Let us learn of him and let him be our light as well—a lamp to our feet and a light to our understanding. May we have the peace that comes from darkness dispelled and the joy that comes of feasting together on his good word.

# CHAPTER SEVENTEEN

# Inviting the Dragon

ONE OF THE GREAT CHALLENGES AND opportunities in life is to learn how to bring more light—particularly the light of Christ—into our lives. Too often fears of different kinds overshadow our lives, and with those fears comes a stultifying darkness. An old Japanese story offers some insights on how we might deal with our fears:

It seems that the people of a certain village were terrorized by a dragon who lived in a cave in the nearby hills. None of them had ever actually *seen* the dragon, but they heard his roaring and passed around stories of him and lived in fear of him.

Imagine the surprise of one mother, then, when her young son announced that he wanted to invite the dragon to his upcoming birthday party! Of course, such a thing was out of the question. But the boy would not be swayed, and he set off up the hill to give his invitation to the dragon.

At first the dragon raged and roared and blew smoke and fire, but the little boy bravely held his ground and described the wonderful party he was going to have. Again and again, he pleaded with the dragon to come.

Finally, the dragon began to believe that the invitation was sincere, and he dissolved into tears at the boy's kindness. The tears made a river, and the dragon was magically transformed into a dragon-steamboat, upon which the boy floated triumphantly home.

213

This story reminds me that each of us, with very few exceptions, has a cave with a dragon in it, somewhere deep inside us. This dragon scares us. It scares us so much that we may not even know it's there anymore. We've pulled such a pile of leaves and grass over it that we can't see it anymore. Whenever we happen to glance that way, we say, "Oh, that's just an old boulder." We whistle when we walk by it.

Our own dragons may take many forms. We may fear being injured in an auto accident. We may suffer from claustrophobia. Perhaps we struggle with sexual abuse experienced as a child. Our fear may be of a physical or sexual addiction that we worry we'll never be free of. It may be the memory of a sin or a crime in our past. It may be a fear of loneliness, a fear of poverty, a fear of old age, a fear of death. We may be haunted by the death of a child or immobilized by the death of a parent or spouse. We may have a fear of never marrying; or even a fear that we *will* marry. For me, the dragon is cancer. I'm a cancer survivor, which, in the statistical game of medicine, means the cancer did not recur within three years after a mastectomy, radiation therapy, and a hysterectomy. Thirteen years later, I had another episode. I live with the daily knowledge that cancer could recur at any time, or appear at another site in my body.

Fears are scary things. They're not imaginary. They're not insignificant or childish overreactions. It's understandable why we fear the accidents and ailments and aggression that remind us how fragile life is and how vulnerable we and the people we love are.

The Lord understands our fears. Do you know how many times the scriptures tell us not to be afraid? According to my count, sixteen times in the Doctrine and Covenants alone and eighty-five times in the Bible. That's a lot of encouragement.

The disciples of Jesus knew something about fear. One of the most terrifying episodes of their lives must have been when they were tossed in the midst of the Sea of Galilee in their little fishing boat, trying fruitlessly to make headway against a contrary wind. Then, exhausted and in danger of their lives, they looked up to see what they thought was a spirit moving toward them over the water. It must have been a moment of sheer terror. Then "Jesus spake unto them, saying, Be of good cheer; it is I; be not afraid." (Matthew 14:27.) And their fear became worship.

What happens to fear if we invite the dragon to our party? What happens if we face it squarely, call it out of its lair, look at it, ignore its roaring, and keep saying, "Please come to my party"? Is it possible that its roar will turn to a healing flood of tears and that it will carry us back home, suddenly shrunk to dragon-boat size? It's likely. But remember, as long as it stays up there in the mountain roaring, we have to huddle in fear in the valleys.

We all have dragons. And sooner or later, I believe, we all have to face them. Let's remember four lessons from the story of the dragon's tears:

First, the little boy voluntarily went to the dragon. Nobody can make the dragon go away for you. You have to do it yourself.

Second, the story doesn't say that the boy wasn't afraid. It's okay to be afraid and to admit it.

Third, the dragon's immediate reaction was to threaten and roar. It was only when the boy persisted in his invitation that the dragon melted into tears. Be prepared to spend time calling out your dragon. It won't happen overnight.

Fourth, the boy succeeded in destroying the dragon as a threat—not by slaying it but by transforming it into something he could live with. It even became a servant to him. A fear transformed can be a great strength to you. If you kill a dragon, you always have to worry whether it might have left its mate somewhere in a deeper cave. If you drive it away, you always have to worry about it coming back. But if you transform it, you have a permanent new relationship with it.

One difference between our lives and the story is that the boy went alone to face his dragon. We don't have to go alone. Most times, we need help in dealing with our fears — the help of a trusted confidant or family member, the expert help of a professional therapist, the sustaining help of an understanding bishop.

When I think of fear — and also of courage — I think of an experience I had when I was six or seven years old. I was afraid of the dark, and nights in Hawaii can be very dark indeed. We lived in a tiny village without street lights, and our house stood on the outskirts of the village. My mother was ill, and one evening she grew much worse. My father said, "Chieko, you must go to the store and get medicine for her." I don't know if my parents knew how I felt about the dark. I had just always arranged to be inside after it got dark without making any comments about it. I knew that they wouldn't ever send me into real danger — but they were adults and I was a child. You know how vulnerable you feel when you're a child and how grown-ups always seem so powerful and strong? Maybe they didn't even see the danger that I sensed so strongly in the shadows.

But I didn't say anything at this time. I could see how ill my mother was. I was the oldest child. I knew I had to go. My father gave me the family flashlight and I set off. We lived on a little dirt lane with thick jungle trees and bushes growing on each side. I walked down the middle of that rutted lane, listening to my own heart beat. Oh, I was scared! I've never been so scared in my life! But I knew I had to go on.

When I reached the village where there was a boardwalk that snaked along over the ground, I jumped on it and ran as fast as I could. The storekeeper lived in the back of his shop so I had no trouble getting the medicine for my mother. I can't remember if the trip back home was as terrifying as the trip to the store or not. I knew it was worth it, though, because I could give my mother the medicine.

Looking back on that experience, I can see that I was lucky. No matter how huge and how paralyzing my fear was, something else was stronger—that combination of love for my mother, my feeling of duty to the family, my respect for my parents that would not let me disobey them no matter how frightened I was. We all need something that strong in our lives. It may be the determination to carry on for our children's sake. It may be our trust in our Heavenly Father. It may be the memory of having faced hard things and succeeded at them. It may be the example of someone else who has gone through something like our own experience and emerged intact. What in your life corresponds to the great need that draws you out into the darkness with the protection of a feeble flashlight, just strong enough to show you the next few steps that you can take? What gift does the darkness have for you? What medicine to bring back to a loved one?

Whenever I think of sources of true courage, I return to the gospel and to the good news that it brings of the Savior's life, love, and atonement. I love this passage in the Doctrine and Covenants: "Now, what do we hear in the gospel which we have received? A voice of gladness! A voice of mercy from heaven; and a voice of truth out of the earth; . . . a voice of gladness for the living and the dead; glad tidings of great joy . . . giving line upon line, precept upon precept; here a little, and there a little; giving us consolation by holding forth that which is to come, confirming our hope! . . . Shall we not go on in so great a cause? Go forward and not backward. Courage, . . . and on, on to the victory!" (D&C 128:19, 21–22.)

Now, there's a message for moments of despondency and discouragement! There's a message that dispels doubt and casts out fear. It is the glad tidings of the gospel, of him who walked through the storm on the Sea of Galilee that dark midnight. The Savior knows about the dragons that lie in their caves deep within us. There is no experience we face that he has not faced before. There is no temptation he has not resisted, no suffering he has not endured, no pain for which his grace is not sufficient.

It is my hope that we will have strength to climb our mountains and face our dragons — to face whatever is preventing us from living the gospel fully and joyously, as Jesus intended that we should. May we call out our dragons and transform them into something we can live with — even something that can serve us. As we go through this frightening process, let us be strengthened by the memory of Jesus' apostles, looking up in danger and facing what they thought was an even greater danger, only to hear the voice of Jesus saying, "It is I; be not afraid."

# Strength in Every Season

THIS SEASON OF MY LIFE—THE SPRING OF 1992—is a difficult one. My husband, Ed, died in March. Just a few weeks later, we lost a grandchild, who died a few days before it was due to be born. And a few weeks after that, my brother was diagnosed as having a cranial tumor This is a season of loss and sorrow for me. And the hardest of all these experiences is the death of my beloved husband. I am moving into a new season, changing roles from wife to widow. The word seems strange to me. The change is strange to me.

Ed came with me to the Relief Society sesquicentennial broadcast on March 14, 1992, in the Tabernacle on Temple Square. I could see him on the front row from my seat on the stand. President Thomas S. Monson told me how he looked down, during my talk, to see Ed beaming up at me, listening to every word with pride and pleasure. Ed came up afterwards to tell me how well I had done, so happy that it had gone smoothly. Looking into his face, I saw something changed about him that made me look twice—a new serenity, a new peacefulness.

After the broadcast, we had a very pleasant lunch together as a Relief Society presidency with our husbands. Afterwards, Ed and I walked back to the Church Office Building parking plaza with Elaine Jack and her husband, Joe.

Suddenly, between one step and another, Ed dropped to the sidewalk. His heart just stopped. Joe Jack, who is a surgeon, instantly began attending to Ed's needs. The Church security personnel, also trained in CPR, came running to help. And the hospital was only a few blocks away. Still, Ed's heart did not stabilize until they had been working on him for some time in the hospital. He never regained consciousness, not even for a moment, and he died six days later.

Looking back on the experience, I truly feel that the Lord took Ed from us gently. He let him share the beautiful experience of the sesquicentennial broadcast. Ed loved how it showed the power of the gospel to unite people from many cultures around the world. We had time to be together afterwards in a pleasant social experience with our close friends and my sisters in the presidency. When Ed's heart failed, it was between one step and the next—instantly and totally—but with a doctor literally beside him and trained personnel only a call away. He received a priesthood blessing within minutes. So we know that everything possible that could have been done for him was done. Because he never regained consciousness, we could accept that it was time for Ed to go. I knew that he would have responded to me and the boys if it had been even remotely within his power. Because he lingered for a few days, Bob and Ken could be with him and we three together had time to absorb that reality slowly instead of having such a terrible shock thrust upon us brutally. Many General Authorities came to visit while we were in the hospital. They blessed Ed. They prayed with us. And none of us could call him back.

This is a season of sorrow for me and my family, but it has also been a season of strength and faith. I discover, now that this time has come to me, that I have been preparing every day for it through every act of faith and service. Less than two weeks after Ed's death, I celebrated the fiftieth anniversary of my baptism in the Church on April 6, 1942. I have had a lifetime of experiencing the love and care of my Heavenly Father, and I felt that love and care surround me and my sons in the hospital.

Ed was one of the most compassionate Christians I have ever known, and as a family we have tried to follow his example. And we have had the opportunity to be on the receiving end as we have felt the compassion and kindness of everyone around us — doctors, nurses, friends, ward and stake members, an increased outpouring of love, if that were possible, from my sisters on the general board and in the general Relief Society presidency, many Relief Society sisters from all over the United States and some from other countries, friends from past Church assignments, former missionaries — the list simply does not end. Elaine Jack stood beside me, her arms around me, on that sidewalk. Aileen Clyde did not leave me at the hospital all that afternoon and far into the night.

I have had a lifetime of building faith in Christ, and hearing the promise in the sacrament prayer: "that they may always have his Spirit to be with them." That prayer is very personal to me now. I need the Spirit of Christ through the Holy Ghost to be with me more now than I ever have, and I feel that promise being literally fulfilled, week by week. You cannot imagine the gratitude I feel, each Sabbath, as I partake of the sacrament, renew the promises I made at baptism, and feel the Savior making an answering promise to me. I cannot find words to tell you how strong and how comforting that sense of companionship is as I go about my duties.

I could put my energy into feeling Ed's loss, and I have had many quiet moments of shedding tears and of mourning. But I want to put my energy where Ed put his — into feeling the strength of Christ's love for us, into serving others out of that love, into showing my gratitude for a Savior who knows us and cares about us, into loving a Heavenly Father who has received Ed to himself again with joy and who strengthens me in the time that remains before we can be together again.

You know, there are many references in the scriptures to seasons. Thirty-two times the scriptures refer to a "due season" or an "appointed season" or a "little season." This tells me that our Heavenly Father knows the seasons of our lives. He knows that there are seasons when it is right that something should happen, such as a season for being a student and concentrating on the joyous challenge of learning, or a season for concentrating on the responsibilities and blessings of motherhood. There are seasons appointed to us for intensive service, as on a mission or in a demanding Church calling. There are little seasons when we need the view of eternity to realize that a moment of tribulation will pass away if we can have the strength to endure it. Seasons come and seasons go.

I have found particular comfort in one scripture, a promise that the Lord made to the entire people of Israel, but that I am applying to myself: "The Lord shall open unto thee his good treasure, the heaven to give the rain unto thy land *in his season*, and to bless all the work of thine hand." (Deuteronomy 28:12; emphasis added.) I feel that openness of the Lord. I feel that outpouring of blessing. I feel the "good treasure" of faith.

All of these meanings of *season* are nouns. But *season* is also a verb. The Savior reminded us of this sense when he said, "Salt is good: but if the salt have lost his saltness, wherewith will ye season it? Have salt in yourselves, and have peace one with another." (Mark 9:50.) This is a time to see if I have that salt in myself, if I am seasoned for the work. I have learned that a crisis tests the strength that you already have. When it comes upon you, it is too late to acquire the strength. Remember the story of the wise and foolish virgins?

In these last few difficult weeks, each part of the fivefold mission statement of the Relief Society has come to have a deeper meaning for me. First, to build personal testimony: These experiences have taught me the depths of the faith I have, and have increased that faith. Second, to bless the individual woman: Many women have reached out to me. The sisterhood I have felt is profound. Third, to develop and exercise charity: I have been the recipient of the pure love of Christ, both directly and as manifest through the sisters of the Church. Fourth, to strengthen families: This has been a powerful but tender time of drawing together for me and my sons and kin from both sides of the family. And fifth, to enjoy a unified sisterhood: I have. I do. There is no strength, no unity, no consolation like that administered by others who share the same hope in the Savior and the same faith in his grace and love.

Many have already suffered and learned the difficult lessons that are just now coming to me. I know there are seasons of adversity and tribulation for each one of us. I tell you lovingly that you can withstand these seasons and grow during them. Do not meet them alone. Meet them from a place you have established for yourself within the circle of the Relief Society sisterhood. Meet them, already experiencing the companionship of Christ. Meet them knowing that the Savior has strength for every season. I feel to say with the Apostle Paul to you: "I have learned this secret, so that anywhere, at any time, I am content, whether I am full or hungry, whether I have too much or too little. I have the strength to face all conditions by the power that Christ gives me." (Philippians 4:11–13, Good News Version.)

With all of my soul, I witness that these things are true.

# Sources

Many of the chapters in this volume were adapted from materials originally delivered as addresses, as follows:

Chapter 1, "Lighten Up!": Oakland, California, May 6, 1991

Chapter 2, "Principles and Practices": Bountiful Mueller Park Stake, April 13, 1991

Chapter 3, "Walk in My Zori": Ricks College Devotional, April 2, 1991

Chapter 4, "Limitations: A Fine Line": Pennsylvania and West Virginia sacrament meetings, May 21, 1991

Chapter 5, "For Such a Time As This": Pittsburgh Pennsylvania East Stake Women's Meeting, May 20–21, 1991

Chapter 6, "A House of Glory": Irvine California Stake Relief Society Conference, March 2, 1991

Chapter 7, "Motherhood: Less Guilt, More Joy": Written as essay.

Chapter 8, "Defining Ourselves": West Virginia Women's Conference, May 22, 1991

Chapter 9, "Three Ideas for a Brighter Life": Denver North Region Women's Conference, October 18–19, 1991

Chapter 10, "The Pure Spirit of Charity": Written as essay.

Chapter 11, "Surrounded by Samaritans": Wells [Salt Lake City] Stake Relief Society Fireside, June 6, 1991

Chapter 12, "The Power of Charity": Sandy East Stake Women's Conference, February 22, 1992

Chapter 13, "Neither Do I Condemn Thee": Pittsburgh Pennsylvania Stake Women's Conference, May 20–21, 1991

Chapter 14, "Opening the Door to Christ": Albuquerque New Mexico Stake Women's Conference, December 7, 1991; Central Utah Region, February 29, 1992

SOURCES

Chapter 15, "Spiritual Preparation": American Falls Idaho Tri-Stake Women's Conference, April 27, 1991

Chapter 16, "Learn of Me": Sacramento California Stake Women's Conference, May 25, 1991

Chapter 17, "Inviting the Dragon": Oakland California Stake Singles Fireside, May 19, 1991

Epilogue, "Strength in Every Season": BYU Women's Conference Panel, May 7, 1992

# Index